sewandgo
TOTES

LEISURE ARTS, INC.
Little Rock, Arkansas

EDITORIAL STAFF

Managing Editor: Susan White Sullivan
Designer Relations Director: Debra Nettles
Quilt Publications Director: Cheryl Johnson
Special Projects Director: Susan Frantz Wiles
Senior Prepress Director: Mark Hawkins
Technical Writer: Jean Lewis
Technical Editor: Lisa Lancaster
Editorial Writer: Susan McManus Johnson
Photostylist: Angela Alexander
Photographer: Jason Masters
Art Publications Director: Rhonda Shelby
Art Category Manager: Lora Puls
Graphic Artists: Dayle Carroza, Angela Stark,
Janie Wright, and Frances Huddleston
Photography Manager: Katherine Atchison
Imaging Technicians: Brian Hall, Stephanie Johnson,
and Mark R. Potter
Publishing Systems Administrator: Becky Riddle
Publishing Systems Assistants: Clint Hanson and
John Rose

BUSINESS STAFF

Vice President and Chief Operations Officer:
Tom Siebenmorgen
Director of Finance and Administration:
Laticia Mull Dittrich
Vice President, Sales and Marketing: Pam Stebbins
National Accounts Director: Martha Adams
Sales and Services Director: Margaret Reinold
Information Technology Director: Hermine Linz
Controller: Francis Caple
Vice President, Operations: Jim Dittrich
Comptroller, Operations: Rob Thieme
Retail Customer Service Manager: Stan Raynor
Print Production Manager: Fred F. Pruss

Library of Congress Control Number: 2008942177
ISBN-13: 978-1-60140-925-6
ISBN-10: 1-60140-925-7

10 9 8 7 6 5 4 3 2 1

sewing's in her
SYSTEM

When Kristine Poor began sewing, it wasn't the fabric that attracted her—it was the sewing machine.

"I was seven years old and loved playing with the sewing machine," Kristine says. "It was fascinating, learning all the things that it could do. I made doll clothes, but they were a secondary interest. The functions of the sewing machine had me completely."

Knowing this, it's no surprise to learn that Kristine grew up to design assembly lines. With her degree in Mechanical Engineering, it was her job to write the instructions for how items would be put together.

By the time she started Poorhouse Quilt Designs in 2006, Kristine was ready to be enchanted by the huge variety of fabrics and specialty threads available to quilters and sewers. Kristine's mom, Jean Johnson, assists by testing and editing the patterns. A visitor to PoorhouseQuiltDesigns.com will find a variety of bags and totes among Kristine's designs, as well as a few quilts.

Kristine says, "Bags are my favorite things to make, because they're 3-D, structural. Seeing the parts work together in a system is still the aspect of sewing that I most enjoy."

do you recognize this
SCENARIO?

She hurries through the house each morning, stuffing gym clothes into a briefcase and cramming lunch into a twelve-pound purse that's bursting at the seams and—(she takes a deep breath)—where is that cell phone?

If that's your life, then you deserve a few hours this weekend to turn your favorite fabrics into a one-of-a-kind handbag, backpack, or oversize duffle that's actually meant to keep up with everything from skateboards to bongo drums and diapers to daily planners. You can also toss these totes into the washer to get rid of that lovely gym sock fragrance (can't do that with a briefcase).

Even if your life is stress-free, a few hours of fun sewing will bag you way more than a week's worth of compliments on your talent. So feel free to get creative, and know that your gear will always be ready when you are.

star sampler TOTE

These stars can be seen day or night, and they're happy to tote your stuff—all of it—around the clock. There are a zillion ways this really roomy, pocket-sided bag can be useful. One of our favs is taking the tote to the supermarket. That way, you don't have to choose between paper or plastic, because thinking green is another stellar idea.

Finished Tote Size: 16" x 14^1/$_2$" x 3^1/$_2$" (41 cm x 37 cm x 9 cm)
Finished Star Blocks Size: 6" x 6" (15 cm x 15 cm)

SUPPLIES
Yardage is based on 43"/44" (109 cm/112 cm) wide fabric.
  2^5/$_8$ yds (2.4 m) of black star print fabric
  ^{1}/$_2$ yd (46 cm) of red tone-on-tone fabric
  ^{1}/$_8$ yd (11 cm) of orange tone-on-tone fabric
  ^{3}/$_8$ yd (34 cm) of orange batik fabric
  ^{1}/$_4$ yd (23 cm) of yellow tone-on-tone fabric
You will also need:
  55" x 25^1/$_2$" (140 cm x 65 cm) rectangle of lightweight batting
    (we used Warm and Natural®)
  ^{5}/$_8$ yd (57 cm) of Pellon® Peltex®70 heavyweight interfacing
  Quilt basting spray

CUTTING THE PIECES

*Follow **Rotary Cutting**, page 72, to cut fabric. Cut all strips across the selvage-to-selvage width of the fabric. All measurements include $^1/_4$" seam allowances.*

From black star print fabric:
- Cut 2 **large rectangles** 23" x 36" (outer tote and tote lining).
- Cut 2 **pocket linings** $23^1/_2$" x $8^1/_2$".
- Cut 2 **handles** $4^1/_2$" x 40".
- Cut 1 strip 3" wide. From this strip, cut 4 **large squares** 3" x 3".
- Cut 1 strip $2^7/_8$" wide. From this strip, cut 8 **medium squares** $2^7/_8$" x $2^7/_8$" and 8 **smallest squares** 2" x 2".
- Cut 2 strips $2^1/_2$" wide. From these strips, cut 24 **small squares** $2^1/_2$" x $2^1/_2$".
- Cut 4 **pocket sashings** 2" x $6^1/_2$".

From red tone-on-tone fabric:
- Cut 2 **handle accents** $2^3/_4$" x 40".
- Cut 2 **binding strips** $2^1/_2$" wide.
- Cut 1 strip $3^1/_2$" wide. From this strip, cut 2 **largest squares** $3^1/_2$" x $3^1/_2$" and 2 **large squares** 3" x 3".

From orange tone-on-tone fabric:
- Cut 1 strip 3" wide. From this strip, cut 2 **large squares** 3" x 3" and 6 **small squares** $2^1/_2$" x $2^1/_2$".

From orange batik fabric:
- Cut 4 **pocket binding strips** 2" x 22".

From yellow tone-on-tone fabric:
- Cut 1 strip $2^1/_2$" wide. From this strip, cut 6 **small squares** $2^1/_2$" x $2^1/_2$".
- Cut 1 strip $1^3/_4$" wide. From this strip, cut 8 **small rectangles** $1^3/_4$" x $3^1/_4$".

From batting:
- Cut 1 **tote batting** 23" x 36".
- Cut 2 **pocket battings** $23^1/_2$" x $8^1/_2$".

From interfacing:
- Cut 4 **handle interfacings** $1^1/_2$" x 20".

PIECING THE BLOCKS

*Follow **Sewing**, page 73, and **Pressing**, page 75. Match right sides and raw edges and use a ¹/₄" seam allowance.*

Ohio Star Block

1. Referring to **Making Triangle-Squares**, page 74, use 4 black star print **small squares** and 4 orange tone-on-tone **small squares** to make 8 **Triangle-Square A's**. Trim Triangle-Squares to 2" x 2".

Triangle-Square A
(make 8)

2. Repeat **Step 1** using 4 black star print **small squares** and 4 yellow tone-on-tone **small squares** to make 8 **Triangle-Square B's**.

Triangle-Square B
(make 8)

3. Sew 4 **Triangle-Square A's**, 4 **Triangle-Square B's**, 4 black star print **smallest squares** and 1 red tone-on-tone **largest square** together to make **Ohio Star Block**. Block should measure 6¹/₂" x 6¹/₂", including seam allowances. Make 2 Ohio Star Blocks.

Ohio Star Block
(make 2)

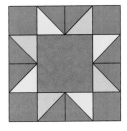

54-40 Star Block

1. Place a dot in the center top edge of 1 black star print **medium square**. Draw a line from center dot to each bottom corner of square (**Fig. 1**). Cut along drawn line to make 1 **center triangle**. Repeat with remaining black star print medium squares to make 8 **center triangles**.

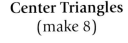

Fig. 1   **Center Triangles**
(make 8)

2. Draw a diagonal line from top left to bottom right corners on 4 yellow tone-on-tone **small rectangles** (**Fig. 2**). Draw a diagonal line from top right to bottom left corners on remaining yellow tone-on-tone **small rectangles** (**Fig. 3**). Cut along drawn lines to make 8 **right side triangles** and 8 **left side triangles**.

Fig. 2   **Fig. 3**

Right Side Triangle   **Left Side Triangle**
(make 8)   (make 8)

          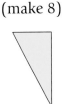

3. Referring to **Fig. 4**, match top points of triangles to sew 1 right side triangle to right side of a center triangle. Repeat to sew 1 left side triangle to left side of center triangle to make a **star point**. Make 8 star points.

Fig. 4

Star Points
(make 8)

4. Sew 4 black star print **small squares**, 4 star points, and 1 orange tone-on-tone **small square** together to make 54-40 Star Block. Block should measure 6¹/₂" x 6¹/₂", including seam allowances. Make 2 54-40 Star Blocks.

54-40 Star Block
(make 2)

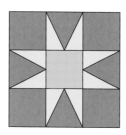

Friendship Star Block

1. Referring to **Making Triangle-Squares**, page 74, use 2 black star print **large squares** and 2 orange tone-on-tone **large squares** to make 4 **Triangle-Square C's.** Trim Triangle-Squares to 2¹/₂" x 2¹/₂".

Triangle-Square C
(make 4)

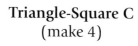

2. Repeat Step 1 using 2 black star print **large squares** and 2 red tone-on-tone **large squares** to make 4 **Triangle-Square D's.**

Triangle-Square D
(make 4)

3. Sew 4 black star print **small squares**, 2 **Triangle-Square C's**, 2 **Triangle-Square D's**, and 1 yellow tone-on-tone **small square** together to make **Friendship Star Block**. Block should measure 6¹/₂" x 6¹/₂", including seam allowances. Make 2 Friendship Star Blocks.

Friendship Star Block
(make 2)

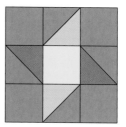

MAKING THE POCKETS

1. Sew 1 **Ohio Star Block**, 1 **54-40 Star Block**, 1 **Friendship Star Block**, and 2 **pocket sashings** together to make **pieced pocket**. Make 2 pieced pockets.

Pieced Pocket
(make 2)

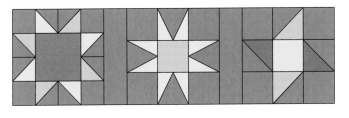

2. Refer to **Making Quilted Fabric**, page 75, to layer and quilt each pocket as desired using **pieced pockets**, **pocket battings**, and **pocket linings**.

Quilting Tip: Our pieced pockets are quilted with an allover meandering pattern.

3. Trim batting and linings even with edges of pieced pockets.
4. Matching wrong sides and raw edges, press **pocket binding strips** in half lengthwise.
5. Refer to **Attaching Open End Binding**, page 78, to bind 1 long edge of each pocket using 1 prepared pocket binding strip. This will be the top of your pockets. Set pockets and remaining pocket binding strips aside.

PREPARING THE HANDLES

1. Cut 1 **handle interfacing** in half to make two $1^1/_2$" x 10" pieces.
2. Place 1 long and 2 short handle interfacings together in the order shown (**Fig. 5**). Butt (do not overlap) short edges against each other and zigzag together. Repeat using remaining handle interfacings.

Fig. 5

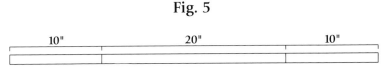

3. Press 1 long edge of **handle** $^5/_8$" to the wrong side.
4. Aligning edge of 1 **handle interfacing** with un-pressed edge of fabric, place interfacing on wrong side of 1 **handle** piece. Stitch in place $^1/_4$" from the edge (**Fig. 6**).

Fig. 6

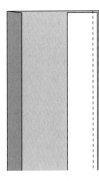

5. Fold interfacing over once, then fold pressed edge of handle over interfacing (**Fig. 7**); pin in place.

Fig. 7

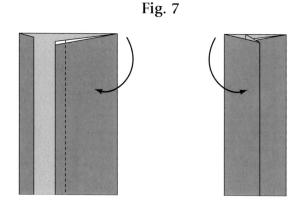

6. Press both long edges of 1 **handle accent** ³/₄" to wrong side.
7. Center and pin 1 handle accent over 1 handle. Topstitch on either side of handle accent close to folded edges of handle accent. Topstitch through center of handle (**Fig. 8**).

Fig. 8

8. Repeat **Steps** 3-7 using remaining handle and handle accent.

ASSEMBLING THE TOTE

1. Refer to **Making Quilted Fabric**, page 75, to layer and quilt as desired using **tote lining large rectangle**, **tote batting**, and **outer tote large rectangle**. Trim quilted fabric to width of pocket x 34" to make **tote body**.

Quilting Tip: Our tote body is quilted with an allover meandering pattern.

2. Position the bound edge of each pocket 4" from each short side of tote body (**Fig. 9**); pin in place. Baste ¹/₄" from the sides and bottom edges of the pockets. This will prevent the pockets from shifting when attaching the handles.

Fig. 9

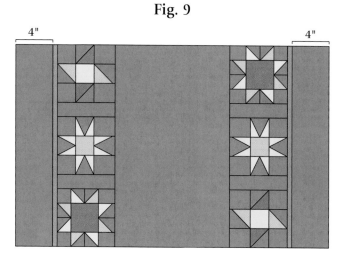

3. Center and pin handles over pocket sashings (**Fig. 10**). Refer to **Fig. 11** to attach handles by topstitching over existing outer topstitching and across handle at top edge of pocket. Topstitch $1/4$" from previous stitching for reinforcement.

Fig. 10

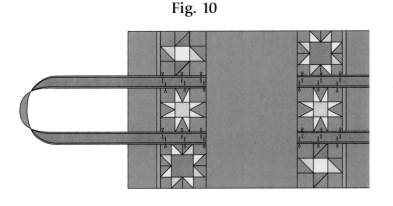

Fig. 11

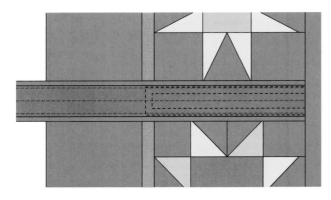

4. Position raw edge of 1 pocket binding strip $1/4$" from bottom raw edge of 1 pocket. Using a $1/4$" seam allowance, stitch binding strip to tote body (**Fig. 12**). Fold binding strip up to cover raw edge of pocket. Topstitch in place. Repeat for remaining pocket. Trim ends of binding even with sides of tote body.

Fig. 12

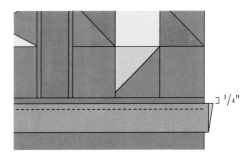

5. Matching outer fabric and short edges, fold tote body in half. Beginning at fold, sew side seams.

6. Refer to **Making Binding**, page 77, to use **binding strips** to make binding.

7. To bind seam allowances, refer to **Attaching Closed End Binding**, page 78, for bottom end of seam allowances and **Attaching Open End Binding**, page 78, for top end of seam allowances. Refer to **Attaching Continuous Binding**, page 77, to bind top edge of tote.

8. To box the bottom, turn tote wrong side out. Match right sides and align tote front/back side seams with center of tote bottom. Refer to **Fig. 13** to sew across point 2" from tip. Repeat for remaining side seam and bottom. Turn right side out.

Fig. 13

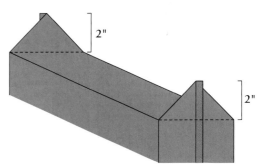

crafty TOTE

Great for transporting everything from pablum to portfolios, this tantalizing tote has another use that's our favorite—making art projects portable! Besides being big enough to hold all your materials, the bag itself is a generous canvas for showing off a selection of bold fabrics. Pack it full of creative tools and head for the park. Like the artwork you'll fashion, this bag is a true original.

Finished Size: 20" x 20" x 5" (51 cm x 51 cm x 13 cm)

SUPPLIES
Yardage is based on 43"/44" (109 cm/112 cm) wide fabric.
- $1^7/_8$ yds (1.7 m) of yellow floral fabric
- $2^3/_8$ yds (2.2 m) blue print fabric
- $^1/_8$ yd (11 cm) **each** of 3 coordinating fabrics for pieced pockets

You will also need:
- 46" x 51" (117 cm x 130 cm) rectangle of lightweight batting (we used Warm and Natural®)
- $1^1/_8$ yds (1 m) of Pellon® Peltex®70 heavyweight interfacing
- Quilt basting spray
- 26" (66 cm) plastic zipper

CUTTING THE PIECES

*Follow **Rotary Cutting**, page 72, to cut fabric. Cut all strips across the selvage-to-selvage width of the fabric. All measurements include seam allowances.*

From yellow floral fabric:
- Cut 1 strip $14^1/2$" wide. From this strip, cut 2 **pocket linings** $14^1/2$" x $14^1/2$".
- Cut 1 **outer fabric** 28" x 47".
- Cut 2 **lower zipper facings** 2" x 26".
- Cut 2 **upper zipper facings** $2^1/4$" x 26".
- Cut 8 **squares** 4" x 4".
- Cut 2 **zipper end covers** $1^1/2$" x $2^1/2$".

From blue print fabric:
- Cut 4 **binding strips** $2^1/2$" wide.
- Cut 2 **handles** $4^1/2$" x 72", pieced as needed.
- Cut 1 **tote lining** 28" x 47".
- Cut 1 **tote bottom** 26" x $9^1/4$".

From *each* of 3 coordinating fabrics:
- Cut 1 strip 4" wide. From this strip, cut 8 **squares** 4" x 4".

From batting:
- Cut 1 **tote batting** 28" x 47".
- Cut 2 **pocket battings** $14^1/2$" x $14^1/2$".

From interfacing:
- Cut 4 **handle interfacings** $1^1/2$" x 36".
- Cut 1 **bottom interfacing** 20" x 5" (optional).

PREPARING THE HANDLES

1. Cut 2 **handle interfacings** in half to make four $1^1/2$" x 18" pieces.
2. Place 1 long and 2 short handle interfacings together in the order shown (**Fig. 1**). Butt (do not overlap) short edges against each other and zigzag together. Repeat using remaining handle interfacings.

Fig. 1

18"   36"   18"

3. Press 1 long edge of each **handle** $3/8$" to the wrong side.
4. Aligning 1 edge of interfacing with unpressed edge of handle, place **handle interfacing** on wrong side of handle. Sew in place $1/4$" from edge (**Fig. 2**).

Fig. 2

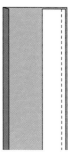

5. Fold interfaced edge over once, then fold pressed edge of fabric over interfaced edge (**Fig. 3**).

Fig. 3

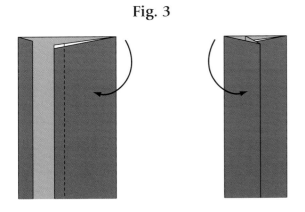

6. Referring to **Fig. 4**, topstitch handle in place close to folded edge. Topstitch at same distance from edge on opposite edge of handle. Topstitch $^1/_8$" outside each topstitching line.

Fig. 4

7. Repeat **Steps 4-6** for remaining handle. Set handles aside.

MAKING THE POCKETS

*Follow **Sewing**, page 73, and **Pressing**, page 75. Match right sides and raw edges and use a $^1/_4$" seam allowance unless otherwise stated.*

1. Referring to **Making Triangle-Squares**, page 74, use 8 yellow floral **squares** and 8 **squares** of one coordinating fabric to make 16 **Triangle-Square A's**. Trim Triangle-Squares A's to $3^1/_2$" x $3^1/_2$".

Triangle-Square A
(make 16)

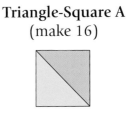

2. Repeat **Step 1** using remaining coordinating fabric **squares** to make 16 **Triangle-Square B's**.

Triangle-Square B
(make 16)

3. Sew 2 **Triangle-Square A's**, and 2 **Triangle-Square B's** together to make **Pinwheel Block**. Make 8 Pinwheel Blocks.

Pinwheel Block
(make 8)

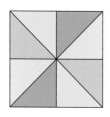

4. Sew 4 Pinwheel Blocks together to make **Pieced Pocket**. Make 2 Pieced Pockets.

Pieced Pocket
(make 2)

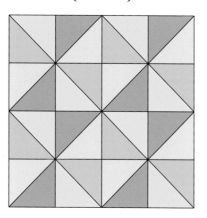

5. Refer to **Making Quilted Fabric**, page 75, to layer and quilt as desired using **pieced pockets**, **pocket linings**, and **pocket battings**.

Quilting Tip: Our pieced pockets are quilted in the ditch along the seamlines.

6. To make **pockets**, trim pocket lining and batting even with edges of pieced pockets.
7. Refer to **Making Binding**, page 77, to use **binding strips** to make **binding**.
8. Refer to **Attaching Open End Binding**, page 78, to bind 1 edge of each pocket. Set pockets and remaining binding aside.

PREPARING THE ZIPPER ASSEMBLY

1. With zipper closed, refer to **Fig. 5** to position short end of 1 **zipper end cover**, right side down, on top of the zipper stop approximately 23" from top of zipper pull. Position remaining **zipper end cover**, right side up, underneath the zipper stop. Sew across zipper and zipper end covers through all layers.

Fig. 5

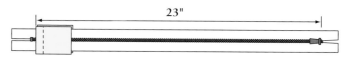

23"

2. Fold zipper end covers to right side and press.
3. Press 1 long edge of each **lower** and **upper zipper facing** $\frac{1}{2}$" to wrong side.
4. With closed zipper wrong side up, position pressed edge of 1 lower zipper facing on zipper tape $\frac{3}{8}$" away from teeth; pin facing in place. Topstitch $\frac{1}{8}$" from folded edge of facing (**Fig. 6**).

Fig. 6

5. With closed zipper right side up, position pressed edge of 1 upper zipper facing over zipper tape and lower facing about $\frac{1}{8}$" away from teeth; pin facing in place. Topstitch $\frac{1}{8}$" from folded edge (**Fig. 7**). Add additional topstitching about $\frac{1}{4}$" and $\frac{1}{8}$" from first topstitching, if desired.

Fig. 7

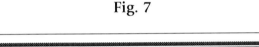

6. Repeat **Steps** 4-5 to sew remaining zipper facings to opposite side of zipper.
7. Baste long raw edges of each pair of zipper facing together.
8. With right side of zipper tucked between layers, fold short ends of zipper facings together. Using a $\frac{1}{2}$" seam allowance, sew across each short end (**Fig. 8**).

Fig. 8

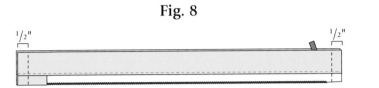

9. To bind each end of **zipper assembly**, refer to **Attaching Closed End Binding**, page 78, to use prepared binding to bind end of seam allowance closest to zipper and **Attaching Open End Binding**, page 78, to bind remaining end. Set zipper assembly aside.

3. Pin handles on either side of pockets, overlapping pockets by $1/4$" (**Fig. 10**). Topstitch in place over outer topstitching.

Fig. 10

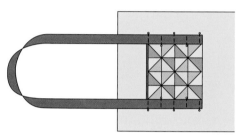

ASSEMBLING THE TOTE

1. Refer to **Making Quilted Fabric**, page 75, to make quilted fabric using **tote lining**, **tote batting**, and **outer fabric**. To make **tote body**, trim quilted fabric to 26" x 45".

Quilting Tip: Our tote body is quilted with an allover diagonal crosshatching pattern.

4. Topstitch a small rectangle on each handle at top of pocket for reinforcement (**Fig. 11**).

Fig. 11

2. With bound edge of pocket facing short edges of tote body, center 1 pocket on each side of tote body, $6^{1}/_{4}$" from the short edges. Pin pockets in place. Baste around sides and bottom of pocket (**Fig. 9**).

Fig. 9

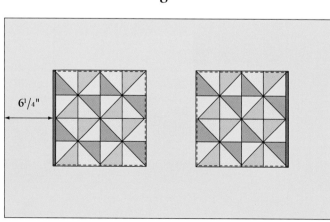

6$^{1}/_{4}$"

5. Press long edges of **tote bottom** $^{1}/_{2}$" to the wrong side.

6. Position tote bottom so that it overlaps unfinished ends of handles and pockets by approximately $^1/_4$". Topstitch in place (**Fig. 12**) along long folded edges; topstitch $^1/_4$" inside previous topstitching.

Fig. 12

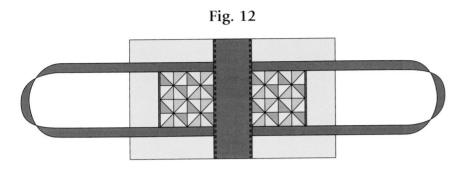

7. Matching outer fabric and short edges, fold tote body in half. Beginning at fold, sew side seams using a $^1/_2$" seam allowance.
8. To bind side seam allowances, use prepared binding and refer to **Attaching Closed End Binding**, page 78, for bottom end of seam allowances and **Attaching Open End Binding**, page 78, for top end of seam allowances.
9. To box bottom, match right sides and align tote front/back side seams with center of tote bottom. Refer to **Fig. 13** to sew across point $2^1/_2$" from tip. Repeat for remaining side seam and bottom. Turn tote right side out.

Fig. 13

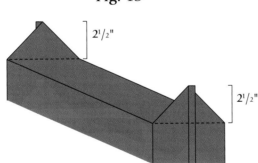

10. To attach zipper assembly, pin zipper assembly inside top raw edge of tote, matching basted edges of zipper facings with top raw edges of tote lining (**Fig. 14**). Sew zipper assembly to tote.

Fig. 14

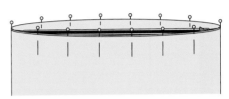

11. Refer to **Attaching Continuous Binding**, page 77, to bind top edge of tote.
12. **Optional:** Cover a 20" x 5" piece of interfacing with leftover fabric and insert it into the bottom of the tote. Glue in place if desired.

mini BAG

Travel light and still take your little necessities: art supplies, cell phone, GPS handheld device (hey, you never know when the urge to go geocaching will strike). Since this itty-bitty bag is quick to make, you should probably have several in different colors.

Finished size: 6$^1/_2$" x 9" x 2$^1/_2$" (17 cm x 23 cm x 6 cm)

SUPPLIES

Yardage is based on 43"/44" (109 cm/112 cm) wide fabric.

  $^1/_4$ yd (23 cm) of blue floral fabric
  $^3/_8$ yd (34 cm) of purple polka dot fabric
  $^3/_8$ yd (34 cm) of lining fabric
  3$^1/_2$" x 3$^1/_2$" (9 cm x 9 cm) square **each** of 3 coordinating fabrics for front flap

You will also need:

  16" x 31" (41 cm x 79 cm) rectangle of lightweight batting (we used Warm and Natural®)
  1$^1/_2$ yds (1.4 m) of $^1/_4$" (6 mm) dia. braided cord for strap
  Quilt basting spray
  Hook and loop closure (optional)

From purple polka dot fabric:
- Cut 2 **binding strips** 2$\frac{1}{2}$" wide.
- Cut 1 **square** 3$\frac{1}{2}$" x 3$\frac{1}{2}$".
- Cut 1 **flap top** 2$\frac{1}{2}$" x 6$\frac{1}{2}$".

From lining fabric:
- Cut 1 **bag lining** 29$\frac{1}{2}$" x 8$\frac{1}{2}$".

From batting:
- Cut 1 **large batting rectangle** 29$\frac{1}{2}$" x 8$\frac{1}{2}$".
- Cut 1 **small batting rectangle** 10" x 6".

MAKING THE FOUR-PATCH BLOCK

*Follow **Sewing**, page 73, and **Pressing**, page 75. Match right sides and raw edges and use a $\frac{1}{4}$" seam allowance.*

1. Sew 2 **squares** together to make **Unit 1**. Make 2 Unit 1's.

Unit 1
(make 2)

2. Sew the 2 Unit 1's together to make a **Four-Patch Block**.

Four-Patch Block

CUTTING THE PIECES

*Follow **Rotary Cutting**, page 72, to cut fabric. Cut all strips across the selvage-to-selvage width of the fabric. All measurements include $\frac{1}{4}$" seam allowances.*

From blue floral fabric:
- Cut 1 strip 6$\frac{1}{2}$" wide. From this strip, cut 1 **outer fabric rectangle** 20" x 6$\frac{1}{2}$" and 1 **bag side rectangle** and 1 **bag side lining rectangle, each** 10" x 6".

MAKING THE MINI BAG SECTIONS

1. Sew **Four-Patch Block, flap top,** and **outer fabric rectangle** together to make **outer bag** (**Fig. 1**). Press seam allowances open.

Fig. 1

2. Refer to **Making Quilted Fabric**, page 75, to layer and quilt as desired using **outer bag**, **large batting rectangle**, and **bag lining**.

Quilting Tip: Our fabric is quilted with an X through the center of the Four-Patch Block. There is outline quilting inside the triangles formed by the X. The flap top is meander quilted and there is diagonal crosshatching on the remainder of the outer bag.

3. Trim backing and batting even with edges of quilted fabric. Trimming length from outer bag end, trim quilted fabric to 27¹/₂" x 6¹/₂" to make **bag body**.
4. Using rounded corner of **Mini Bag side pattern**, page 68, as a guide, trim both corners of the Four-Patch Block end of bag body (**Fig. 2**).

Fig. 2

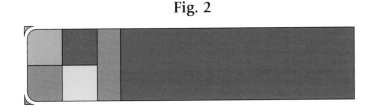

5. Refer to **Making Binding**, page 77, to use **binding strips** to make binding. Set binding aside.
6. To bind short *straight* edge of bag body, use binding and follow **Attaching Open End Binding**, page 78.
7. Make quilted fabric in the same manner as above, using **bag side rectangle**, **small batting rectangle**, and **bag side lining rectangle**.

Quilting Tip: Our fabric is quilted with an allover meandering pattern.

8. Using **Mini Bag side pattern**, page 68, cut 2 **bag sides** from quilted fabric (**Fig. 3**).

Fig. 3

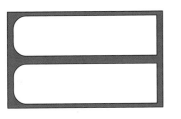

ASSEMBLING THE MINI BAG

1. Referring to **Fig. 4**, mark center bottom of bag body with dots placed 9³/₄" from bound edge and ¹/₄" from each side edge (**Fig. 4**).

Fig. 4

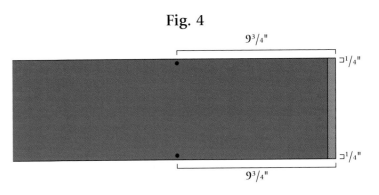

2. Mark center bottom of each bag side with a dot (**Fig. 5**).

Fig. 5

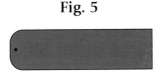

3. On lining side, pin 1 raw end of **strap** to center of each straight raw edge of bag side; stitch across strap ends ¹/₄" below raw edges (**Fig. 6**).

Fig. 6

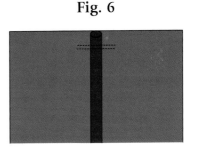

4. To bind short *straight* edges of bag sides using prepared binding, follow **Attaching Open End Binding**, page 78.
5. With lining sides together and matching dots, sew sides to bag body.
6. To bind seam allowances along side, flap, and remaining side using prepared binding, begin at top edge of bag opening and follow **Attaching Closed End Binding**, page 78.
7. **Optional:** Attach hook and loop fastener to flap and bag body.

around town
• • • • • • TOTE

As you dash between destinations, this colorful tote will keep up with you. It's the right size for carrying mail, DVDs, small packages, sunglasses, car keys—all the stuff you need for your weekly tasks. The outer pocket is a perfect place to make your mark with embroidery. This is also a great design to make for gifts.

Finished size: 11" x 11" x 3" (28 cm x 28 cm x 8 cm)
Monograms are everywhere—and it's so easy to add your personal touch to this tote! Our bag features a machine embroidered monogram but you may choose to hand embroider your design. You might even want to use quick and easy purchased iron-on letters to embellish your bag!

SUPPLIES
Yardage is based on 43"/44" (109 cm/112 cm) wide fabric.
   $^1/_2$ yd (46 cm) pink/orange floral fabric
   $1^1/_4$ yds (1.1 m) pink polka dot fabric
   $^1/_2$ yd (46 cm) pink print fabric
   $^1/_8$ yd (11 cm) white/pink floral fabric
   $^1/_4$ yd (23 cm) orange print fabric
   $^3/_8$ yd (34 cm) yellow polka dot fabric
You will also need:
   $21^1/_2$" x 45" (55 cm x 114 cm) rectangle of lightweight batting
    (we used Warm and Natural®)
   Stabilizer (optional)
   11" x $2^3/_4$" (28 cm x 7 cm) piece of Pellon® Peltex®70 heavyweight
    interfacing (optional)
   Quilt basting spray

CUTTING THE PIECES

*Follow **Rotary Cutting**, page 72, to cut fabric. Cut all strips across the selvage-to-selvage width of the fabric. All measurements include seam allowances.*

From pink/orange floral fabric:
- Cut 2 **tote tops** 15" x 5".
- Cut 2 **pocket linings** $8^1/2$" x $8^1/2$".

From pink polka dot fabric:
- Cut 1 **tote lining** $30^1/2$" x 17".
- Cut 1 **tote bottom** 15" x $7^1/2$".
- Cut 2 strips 1" wide. From these strips, cut 4 **pocket sashings** 1" x $6^1/2$" and 1 **narrow pocket strip** 1" x 28".
- Cut 2 **handles** 4" x 43", pieced as needed.

From pink print fabric:
- Cut 1 strip $2^1/2$" wide. From this strip, cut 2 **trim strips** $2^1/2$" x 15".
- Cut 4 **bias strips** $2^1/2$" x 25".

From white/pink floral fabric:
- Cut 2 strips $1^1/2$" wide. From these strips, cut 4 **pocket rectangles** $1^1/2$" x $3^1/2$" and 1 **wide pocket strip** $1^1/2$" x 28".

From orange print fabric:
- Cut 2 **tote middles** 15" x $6^1/2$".

From yellow polka dot fabric:
- Cut 2 **squares** 9" x 9".

From batting:
- Cut 2 **handle battings** $1^1/4$" x 43."
- Cut 1 **tote batting** $30^1/2$" x 17".
- Cut 2 **pocket battings** $8^1/2$" x $8^1/2$".

PREPARING THE TOTE BODY

*Follow **Sewing**, page 73, and **Pressing**, page 75. Match right sides and raw edges and use a $^1/_4$" seam allowance unless otherwise stated.*

1. Matching long edges, sew 1 **tote middle** to each side of **tote bottom**. Sew 1 **tote top** to each tote middle to make **outer tote** (**Fig. 1**). Press seam allowances open.

Fig. 1

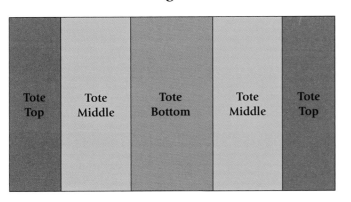

2. Refer to **Making Quilted Fabric**, page 75, to layer and quilt as desired using **tote lining**, **tote batting**, and **outer tote**.

Quilting Tip: Our fabric is quilted with diagonal crosshatching on the tote bottom and allover meander quilting on the remainder of the outer tote.

3. To make **tote body**, trim quilted fabric to $27^1/_2$" x $14^1/_2$". Use **Around Town front/back pattern**, page 71, to cut curved top edges of tote body (**Fig. 2**). Set tote body aside.

Fig. 2

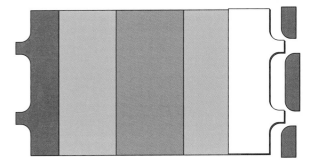

4. Refer to **Making Binding**, page 77, to use **bias strips** to make binding.

5. To bind top curved edges of tote, refer to **Attaching Open End Binding**, page 78. To bind short straight top edges, refer to **Attaching Closed End Binding**, page 78 (**Fig. 3**).

Fig. 3

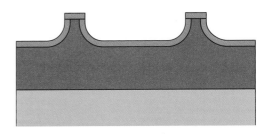

MAKING THE POCKETS

1. Hand or machine embroider or attach a monogram of your choosing on each **square**.

2. Centering monogram, trim embroidered squares to $3^1/_2$" x $3^1/_2$". Set squares aside.

3. To make **Strip Set**, match long edges and sew **narrow** and **wide pocket strips** together. Press seam allowances towards darker fabric.

Strip Set

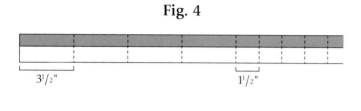

4. Cut across Strip Set as shown in **Fig. 4** to make 4 **Unit 1's** that measure $3^1/2$" x 2" and 8 **Unit 2's** that measure $1^1/2$" x 2".

Fig. 4

Unit 1
(make 4)

Unit 2
(make 8)

5. Sew 1 **Unit 1** to 2 opposite sides of 1 monogrammed square to make **Unit 3**. Make 2 Unit 3's.

Unit 3
(make 2)

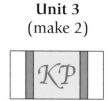

6. Matching short edges, sew 1 **Unit 2** to either side of 1 **pocket rectangle** to make **Unit 4**. Make 4 Unit 4's.

Unit 4
(make 4)

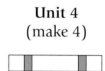

7. Refer to **Pocket Assembly Diagram** to sew 1 Unit 3, 2 **pocket sashings**, and 2 Unit 4's together to make **pieced pocket**. Make 2 pieced pockets.

Pocket Assembly

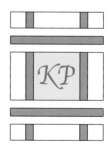

Pieced Pocket
(make 2)

8. Refer to **Making Quilted Fabric**, page 75, to layer and quilt as desired using **pocket linings**, **pocket battings**, and **pieced pockets**.

Quilting Tip: Our pieced pockets are quilted in the ditch between each of the pink sashings.

9. To make **pockets**, trim pocket lining and batting even with pieced pockets.
10. Refer to **Attaching Open End Binding**, page 78, to use prepared binding to bind top edges of pockets. Set pockets and remaining binding aside.

PREPARING THE HANDLES

1. Press 1 long edge of 1 **handle** ¹/₂" to wrong side.
2. Aligning 1 edge of batting with unpressed edge of handle, place **handle batting** on wrong side of handle. Sew in place ¹/₄" from edge (**Fig. 5**).

Fig. 5

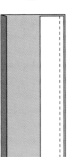

3. Fold batting over once, then fold pressed edge of handle over batting (**Fig. 6**); pin in place.

Fig. 6

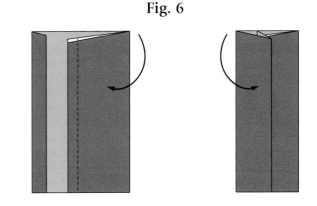

4. Referring to **Fig. 7**, topstitch handle in place close to folded edge. Topstitch along length of opposite side of handle. Topstitch ¹/₈" outside each topstitching line.

Fig. 7

5. Repeat **Steps 1-4** for remaining handle. Set handles aside.

ASSEMBLING THE TOTE

1. Placing bottom raw edge of pocket $1/4$" below seamline between middle and bottom sections, center pocket on tote body; pin. Baste around sides and bottom of pocket.

2. Matching wrong sides and long edges, fold **trim strips** in half; press. Align raw edges of 1 trim strip (facing top of tote) with bottom raw edge of pocket. Sew trim strip to tote body through all layers (**Fig. 8**).

3. Position 1 handle on either side of pocket, overlapping pockets by $1/4$" and covering raw edges (**Fig. 9**); pin handle in place.

Fig. 9

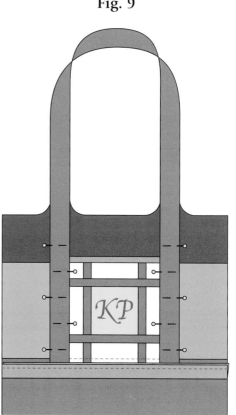

Fig. 8

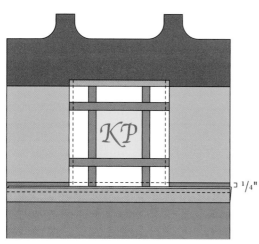

4. Refer to **Fig. 10** to topstitch handle in place over outer topstitching and across top of each handle for reinforcement.

Fig. 10

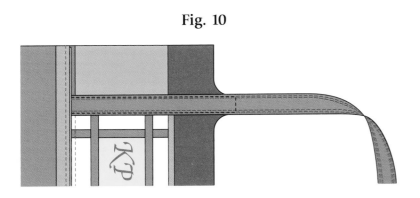

5. Fold trim strip up to cover the bottom raw edges of pocket and handle. Topstitch close to folded edge of trim strip.
6. Repeat **Steps 1-5** to attach remaining pocket, handle, and trim strip to opposite side of tote body.
7. Matching right sides and top edges, fold tote body in half. Using a $1/2$" seam allowance, sew side seams.
8. To bind side seam allowances, refer to **Attaching Closed End Binding**, page 78, and use prepared binding for bottom end of seam allowances and **Attaching Open End Binding**, page 77, for top end of seam allowances.

9. To box bottom, match right sides and align tote front/back side seam with center of tote bottom. Refer to **Fig. 11** to sew across point $1^1/2$" from tip. Repeat for remaining side seam allowance and bottom.

Fig. 11

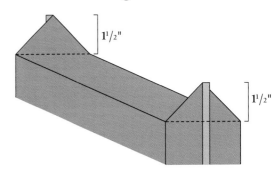

10. **Optional:** Cover a 11" x $2^3/4$" piece of interfacing with leftover fabric and insert it into the bottom of the tote. Glue in place if desired.

quilted
WALLET

Of course, the functions of a wallet need no explanation, so we just want to share this moment with you while you admire the summertime colors of this very useful project. Kind of reminds one of going on a quilting cruise to a tropical destination, doesn't it? Well, wherever you go, the zippered change pocket, credit card and bill pockets, and hook-and-loop closure will keep your valuables secure.

Finished Size: 4" x 5" x 1" (10 cm x 13 cm x 3 cm) when closed,
12" x 5" (30 cm x 13 cm) when open

SUPPLIES
Yardage is based on 43"/44" (109 cm x 112 cm) wide fabric.
- 8" x 9" (20 cm x 23 cm) rectangle **each** of 3 different fabrics for patchwork
- ¼ yd (23 cm) of orange polka dot fabric for lining and zippered pocket
- ¼ yd (23 cm) of pink check fabric for credit card and bill pockets
- ⅛ yd (11 cm) of pink polka dot fabric for binding

You will also need:
- 12½" x 5" (32 cm x 13 cm) rectangle of Pellon® Peltex®71 heavyweight fusible interfacing
- 8" x 20" (20 cm x 51 cm) rectangle of medium weight fusible interfacing
- 2" (5 cm) piece of hook and loop fastener
- 6" (15 cm) plastic zipper

CUTTING THE PIECES

*Follow **Rotary Cutting**, page 72, to cut fabric. Cut all strips across the selvage-to-selvage width of the fabric. All measurements include $^1/4$" seam allowances.*

From *each* patchwork fabric:
- Cut 3 **strips** 2" x 7".

From orange polka dot fabric:
- Cut 1 **lining** $12^1/2$" x 5".
- Cut 1 **zippered pocket top** $2^1/2$" x 5".
- Cut 1 **zippered pocket bottom** 5" x 5".

From pink check fabric:
- Cut 1 **credit card and bill pocket** $18^1/2$" x $4^3/4$".
- Cut 1 **credit card and bill pocket lining** $8^1/2$" x $4^3/4$".

From pink polka dot fabric:
- Cut 1 **binding strip** $2^1/2$" wide.

From medium weight fusible interfacing:
- Cut 1 **credit card and bill pocket interfacing** $4^3/4$" x $18^1/2$".
- Cut 1 **zippered pocket top interfacing** 1" x 5".
- Cut 1 **zippered pocket bottom interfacing** 2" x 5".

Follow Sewing, page 73, and Pressing, page 75. Match right sides and raw edges and use a ¹/₄" seam allowance.

1. Designate **strips** as fabric A, B, and C. Sew strips A-B-C, B-C-A, and C-A-B together to make Strip Sets (**Fig. 1**). Press.

Fig. 1

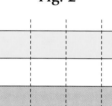

2. Cut across each Strip Set to make three 2" segments (**Fig. 2**). Discard 1 segment.

Fig. 2

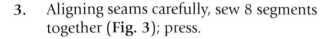

3. Aligning seams carefully, sew 8 segments together (**Fig. 3**); press.

Fig. 3

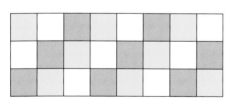

4. Fuse patchwork to **heavyweight interfacing rectangle**.

5. Refer to **Machine Quilting Methods**, page 76, to quilt as desired.

Quilting Tip: Our patchwork rectangle is quilted with an allover meandering pattern.

6. Sew loop side of hook and loop fastener to patchwork as shown in **Fig. 4**. Set patchwork aside.

Fig. 4

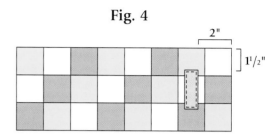

PREPARING ZIPPERED POCKET

1. Matching wrong sides, press **zippered pocket top** in half lengthwise; unfold. With wrong side of zippered pocket top facing up, align 1 edge of **zippered pocket top interfacing** with fold; fuse.

2. Matching wrong sides, press **zippered pocket bottom** in half lengthwise; unfold. With wrong side of zippered pocket bottom facing up, align 1 edge of **zippered pocket bottom interfacing** with fold; fuse.

3. Align folded edges of zippered pocket top and zippered pocket bottom with zipper teeth. Using a zipper foot, topstitch ¹/₈" from folded edges (**Fig. 5**).

Fig. 5

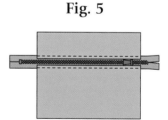

4. Stitch ¹/₄" from edges around zippered pocket, sewing over ends of zipper. Trim zipper even with edges of pocket.

5. Press lower edges of pocket bottom ¹/₄" to wrong side.

PREPARING CREDIT CARD AND BILL POCKET

1. Fuse **credit card and bill pocket interfacing** to wrong side of **credit card and bill pocket**.
2. Referring to **Fig. 6**, insert pins to mark the following measurements on right side of pocket:

Fig. 6

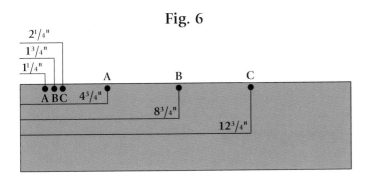

3. Bring location marked A on right to location marked A on left and pin. Repeat for locations B and C to form 3" pockets for credit cards (**Fig. 7**); press. Baste $^1/_4$" from edges along each side.

Fig. 7

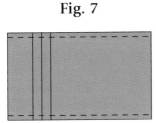

4. With right sides together, sew **credit card and bill pocket** to **credit card and bill pocket lining** along 2 sides (**Fig. 8**).

Fig. 8

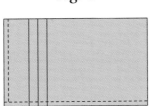

5. Turn right side out and press.

WALLET ASSEMBLY

1. With right sides facing up, pin zippered pocket and credit card and bill pocket to **lining**. Topstitch folded edge of zippered pocket to lining along edge; topstitch again $^1/_4$" from edge. Topstitch left edge of credit card and bill pocket along left edge; topstitch again $^1/_4$" from edge (**Fig. 9**).

Fig. 9

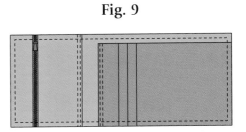

2. Sew hook side of hook and loop fastener to zippered pocket as shown in **Fig. 10**.

Fig. 10

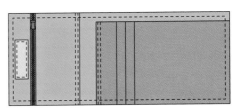

3. Pin lining (right side up) to patchwork (right side down). Baste $^1/_4$" from raw edges.
4. **Optional:** Use rounded corner of the **Mini Bag side pattern**, page 68, to round corners of zippered pocket end of wallet.
5. Matching wrong sides, press binding strip in half lenghtwise. Refer to **Attaching Continuous Binding**, page 77, and **Attaching Binding With Mitered Corners**, page 79, to bind edges.

shoulder BAG

Adjustable shoulder strap, handy side pocket, interior pocket for smaller items, gerbera daisies dotting a sunny background: Be sure to make an extra one of these beauties for your friends to borrow, because you know they're going to ask. Also looks fabulous in the fabric of your choice.

Finished Size: 12" x 9^1/$_2$" x 2" (30 cm x 24 cm x 5 cm)

SUPPLIES

Yardage is based on 43"/44" (109 cm/112 cm) wide fabric.

  1^7/$_8$ yds (1.7 m) of yellow floral fabric

  8" x 8" (20 cm x 20 cm) piece of yellow print fabric for star points

  6" x 3" (15 cm x 8 cm) piece of orange print fabric for star centers

  ^{1}/$_8$ yd (11 cm) of pink print fabric

You will also need:

  31^1/$_2$" x 28" (80 cm x 71 cm) rectangle of lightweight batting (we used Warm and Natural®)

  12^1/$_2$" x 14" (32 cm x 36 cm) rectangle of lightweight fusible interfacing

  ^{1}/$_8$ yd (11 cm) of Pellon® Peltex®70 heavyweight interfacing

  Two 1^1/$_2$" (3.8 cm) D rings

  9" (23 cm) plastic zipper

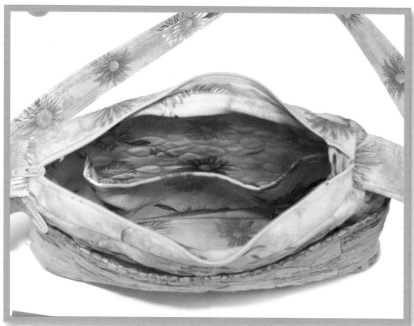

CUTTING THE PIECES

*Follow **Rotary Cutting**, page 72, to cut fabric. Cut all strips across the selvage-to-selvage width of the fabric. All measurements include $1/4$" seam allowances.*

From yellow floral fabric:
- Cut 1 **lining** 26" x 20".
- Cut 1 **pocket lining** $14^1/2$" x $9^1/2$".
- Cut 2 **front/back rectangles** 13" x 11".
- Cut 1 **inner pocket** $12^1/2$" x 14".
- Cut 1 **long strap** $4^1/2$" x $38^5/8$".
- Cut 1 **short strap** $4^1/2$" x $14^7/8$".
- Cut 2 **upper zipper facings** $1^3/8$" x 11".
- Cut 2 **lower zipper facings** $1^1/4$" x 11".
- Cut 1 **bottom rectangle** $3^1/2$" x 12".
- Cut 6 **small squares** 2" x 2".
- Cut 8 **medium squares** $2^1/2$" x $2^1/2$".
- Cut 8 **large squares** $2^7/8$" x $2^7/8$".
- Cut 5 **bias binding strips** $2^1/2$" x 18".

From yellow print fabric:
- Cut 8 **rectangles** $1^3/4$" x $3^1/4$".

From orange print fabric:
- Cut 2 **medium squares** $2^1/2$" x $2^1/2$".

From pink print fabric:
- Cut 1 **pocket binding strip** 2" x 13".
- Cut 6 **small squares** 2" x 2".

From batting:
- Cut 1 **batting rectangle** 26" x 20".
- Cut 1 **pocket batting** $14^1/2$" x $9^1/2$".

From heavyweight interfacing:
- Cut 2 **long strap interfacings** $1^1/4$" x 19".
- Cut 1 **short strap interfacing** $1^1/4$" x $14^1/4$".

MAKING THE OUTER POCKET

*Follow **Sewing**, page 73, and **Pressing**, page 75. Match right sides and raw edges and use a ¹/₄" seam allowance.*

Triangle-Square Strip

1. Referring to **Making Triangle-Squares**, page 74, use 6 yellow floral **small squares** and 6 pink print **small squares** to make 12 **Triangle-Squares**. Trim Triangle-Squares to 1¹/₂" x 1¹/₂".

Triangle-Square
(make 12)

2. Sew 6 Triangle-Squares together to form a **Triangle-Square Strip**. Make 2 Triangle-Square Strips. Set Triangle-Square Strips aside.

Triangle-Square Strip
(make 2)

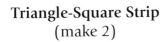

Star Block

1. Mark a dot at center top edge of 1 yellow floral **large square**. Draw a line from center dot to each bottom corner of square (**Fig. 1**). Cut along drawn line to make 1 **center triangle**. Repeat with remaining large squares to make 8 center triangles.

Fig. 1

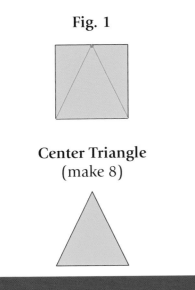

Center Triangle
(make 8)

2. Draw a diagonal line from top left to bottom right corners on 4 yellow print **rectangles** (**Fig. 2**). Draw a diagonal line from top right to bottom left corners on remaining yellow print **rectangles** (**Fig. 3**). Cut along drawn lines to make 8 **right side triangles** and 8 **left side triangles**.

Fig. 2   **Fig. 3**

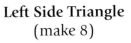

Right Side Triangle   **Left Side Triangle**
(make 8)   (make 8)

   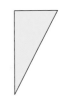

3. Referring to **Fig. 4**, match top points of triangles to sew 1 right side triangle to 1 center triangle. Repeat to sew 1 left side triangle to opposite side of center triangle to make a **star point**. Make 8 star points.

Fig. 4

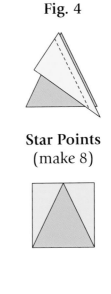

Star Points
(make 8)

4. Sew 4 yellow floral **medium squares**, 4 star points, and 1 orange print **medium square** together to make **Star Block**. Make 2 Star Blocks.

Star Block
(make 2)

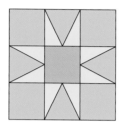

5. Sew 1 **Triangle-Square Strip** to 1 edge of each Star Block (**Fig. 5**).

Fig. 5

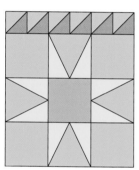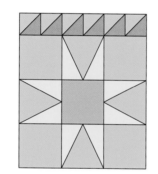

6. Referring to **Fig. 6** for orientation, sew Star Blocks together to make **front pocket**.

Fig. 6

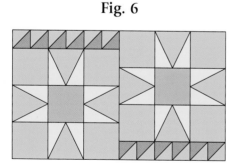

7. Refer to **Making Quilted Fabric**, page 75, to layer and quilt as desired using **front pocket**, **pocket batting**, and **pocket lining**.

Quilting Tip: Our front pocket is quilted in the ditch along all the seamlines. There is an X quilted across the center of each star.

8. Trim batting and lining even with edges of front pocket.
9. Matching wrong sides and raw edges, press **pocket binding strip** in half lengthwise.
10. Refer to **Attaching Open End Binding**, page 78, to bind 1 long edge of front pocket using pocket binding strip. This will be the top of your front pocket. Set front pocket aside.

PREPARING THE QUILTED SECTIONS

1. Refer to **Making Quilted Fabric**, page 75, to layer and quilt as desired using **front/back** and **bottom rectangles, batting rectangle,** and **lining** (**Fig. 7**).

Fig. 7

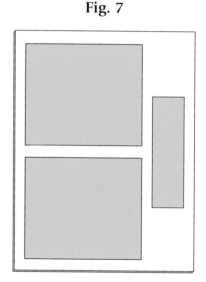

Quilting Tip: Our fabric is quilted with an allover meandering pattern.

2. Trim each front/back rectangle to 12¹/₂" x 10¹/₂". Use **Shoulder Bag front/back pattern**, page 69, to trim top and side edges of 1 front/back rectangle to make **front (Fig. 8)**. Repeat for remaining front/back rectangle to make **back**.

Fig. 8

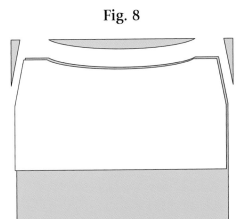

3. Matching wrong side of pocket to right side of front, align raw edges of front pocket with bottom and side edges of front. Baste around pocket, ¹/₄" from side and bottom edges. Beginning with backstitching at bound edge of pocket, stitch in the ditch between Star Blocks to make 2 pocket sections.
4. Use **Shoulder Bag bottom pattern**, page 70, to cut 1 **bottom** from bottom rectangle.
5. Set front, back, and bottom aside.

PREPARING THE INNER POCKET

1. Fuse **lightweight fusible interfacing rectangle** to wrong side of **inner pocket**.
2. Matching wrong sides and short edges, fold inner pocket in half; press.
3. Press folded edge over ³/₈" to one side and topstitch in place. The topstitched side will be the right side of inner pocket.
4. Matching lining side of back and wrong side of pocket, place inner pocket on back. Align long and short raw edges of inner pocket with bottom and side edges of back. Sew inner pocket to back ¹/₄" from sides and bottom edges (**Fig. 9**).

Fig. 9

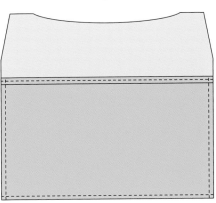

PREPARING THE ZIPPER ASSEMBLY

1. Press 1 long edge of each **lower** and **upper zipper facing** ¹/₂" to wrong side.
2. With closed zipper wrong side up, position pressed edge of 1 lower zipper facing on zipper tape ¹/₄" away from teeth; pin facing in place. Topstitch ¹/₈" from folded edge of facing (**Fig. 10**).

Fig. 10

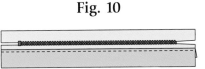

3. With closed zipper right side up, position pressed edge of 1 upper zipper facing over zipper tape and lower facing about 1/8" away from teeth; pin facing in place. Topstitch 1/8" from folded edge (**Fig. 11**).

Fig. 11

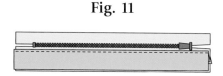

4. Repeat **Steps 2-3** to sew remaining zipper facings to opposite side of zipper to make **zipper assembly**.
5. Referring to **Fig. 12**, trim zipper assembly to 10" long as shown. Set zipper assembly aside.

Fig. 12

10"

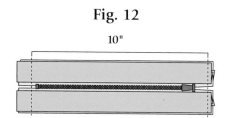

PREPARING THE STRAPS

1. Press 1 long and 1 short edge of **long** and **short strap** 5/8" to wrong side.
2. Cut 1 long strap interfacing in half to make two 1 1/2" x 9 1/2" pieces.
3. Arrange 1 long and 2 short interfacing pieces together as shown. Butt (do not overlap) short edges and zigzag ends together (**Fig. 13**).

Fig. 13

9 1/2"   19"   9 1/2"

4. On wrong side of long strap, align 1 long edge of 1 **long strap interfacing** with long un-pressed edge of strap. Tuck 1 short end of interfacing under folded short end. Stitch in place 1/4" from long edge (**Fig. 14**).

Fig. 14

5. Fold interfacing over once, then fold pressed edge of fabric over interfacing (**Figs. 15-16**).

Fig. 15   **Fig. 16**

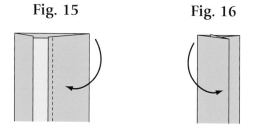

6. Beginning and ending at short raw end, topstitch handle close to folded edge along both long edges and across short finished edge of handle. Topstitch again 1/8" on either side of first topstitching line (**Fig. 17**).

Fig. 17

7. Repeat **Steps 4-6** using short strap and short strap interfacing.
8. Attach D-rings to long strap by placing finished end of strap through D-rings. Fold end of strap 1 3/4" to the wrong side and topstitch in place (**Fig. 18**). Set straps aside.

Fig. 18

ASSEMBLING THE TOTE

1. Refer to **Making Binding**, page 77, to use **bias binding strips** to make **binding**. Set binding aside.

2. Matching right sides, sew raw end of long strap to zipper pull end of zipper assembly. Sew raw end of short strap to opposite end of zipper assembly (**Fig. 19**).

Fig. 19

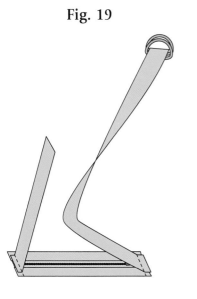

3. Matching right sides and easing as needed, sew 1 edge of zipper assembly to curved top edge of back (**Fig. 20**). Sew remaining side of zipper assembly to curved top edge of front.

Fig. 20

4. Refer to **Attaching Open End Binding**, page 78, to use prepared binding to bind curved top edge seam allowances.

5. Matching right sides and tucking straps between layers, sew front and back together along side edges (**Fig. 21**). Refer to **Attaching Open End Binding**, page 78, to use prepared binding to bind side seam allowances.

Fig. 21

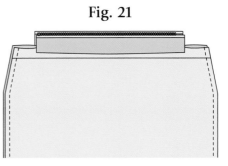

6. Matching right sides, align center of zipper assembly with side seam (**Fig. 22**); sew across end.

Fig. 22

7. Refer to **Attaching Closed End Binding**, page 78, to use prepared binding to bind strap end seam allowances, enclosing upper raw end of side seam allowance in binding.

8. To attach **bottom**, match right sides and align dots on **bottom** with side seams on lower edge of bag body; pin (**Fig. 23**). Easing as needed, sew bottom to bag body.

Fig. 23

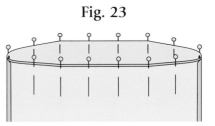

9. Refer to **Attaching Continuous Binding**, page 77, to use prepared binding to bind bottom seam allowances. Turn bag right side out.

floral stripe
BACKPACK

They're not just for schoolbooks and trail mix anymore, but if that's why you want a backpack, this classic bag can take care of those jobs, too. Details include a drawstring and flap closure, handy finger loop, and D-ring straps. There's even an inner pocket for items that need extra stability, like water bottles or small electronics.

Finished Size: 10" x 15" x 6" (25 cm x 38 cm x 15 cm)

SUPPLIES
Yardage is based on 43"/44" (109 cm/112 cm) wide fabric.
  1^1/$_2$ yds (1.4 m) of floral stripe fabric*
  1^1/$_2$ yds (1.4 m) of blue polka dot fabric
  ^{7}/$_8$ yd (80 cm) of green tone-on-tone fabric
You will also need:
  32^1/$_2$" x 38" (83 cm x 97 cm) rectangle of lightweight batting
   (we used Warm and Natural®)
  ^{3}/$_8$ yd (34 cm) of Pellon® Peltex®70 heavyweight interfacing
  Quilt basting spray
  Four 1^1/$_2$" (3.8 cm) D rings
  ^{3}/$_4$ yd (69 cm) of ^{1}/$_4$" (6 mm) dia. twisted cord for drawstring
  Tape in a color to match drawstring cord
  Two 1" (25 mm) long cord stops

* We used a fabric with a combination of wide and narrow print and solid stripes. For the front/side of our bag, we cut a length of fabric that included 1 wide and 2 narrow stripes. For the flap we cut a length that included 1 medium and 2 narrow stripes. Because the stripe lengths are sewn to the top of the bag fabric for decorative purposes only, your lengths can be cut wider or narrower depending on the width and number of stripes you want to feature. For the casings, we cut lengths of the narrow stripe. You will need to cut a section of fabric wide enough for the cord to fit through the casings.

CUTTING THE PIECES

*Follow **Rotary Cutting**, page 72, to cut fabric. Cut all strips across the selvage-to-selvage width of the fabric. All measurements include $1/4$" seam allowances.*

From floral stripe fabric:
- Cut 1 **front/side accent** 24" x desired stripe width + $1/4$" seam allowance on each long edge.
- Cut 1 **flap accent** 11" x desired stripe width + $1/4$" seam allowance on each long edge.
- Cut 1 **front/side/bottom lining** 26" x $23^1/2$".
- Cut 1 **flap lining** 13" x $13^1/2$".
- Cut 2 **long casings** 12" x 2", cut on desired stripe.
- Cut 1 **short casing** $1^1/2$" x 2", cut on desired stripe.
- Cut 1 **loop** 6" x 1".

From blue polka dot fabric:
- Cut 1 **bottom** 11" x $6^3/4$".
- Cut 1 **back** 11" x $14^1/2$".
- Cut 1 **flap** 11" x $11^1/2$".
- Cut 2 **strap covers** 5" x 3".
- Cut 1 **inner pocket** 7" x 18".
- Cut 2 **lower straps** $20^5/8$" x $4^1/2$".
- Cut 1 **front/side** 24" x 15".
- Cut 2 **upper straps** $22^5/8$" x $4^1/2$".

From green tone-on-tone fabric:
- Cut 1 **back lining** 13" x $16^1/2$".
- Cut 2 **front trim strips** 24" x 2".
- Cut 2 **flap trim strips** 11" x 2".
- Cut 1 **back trim strip** 11" x $3/4$".
- Cut 4 **binding strips** $2^1/2$" wide.

From batting:
- Cut 1 **front/side/bottom batting** 26" x $23^1/2$".
- Cut 1 **flap batting** 13" x $13^1/2$".
- Cut 1 **back batting** 13" x $16^1/2$".

From interfacing:
- Cut 2 **lower strap interfacings** 20" x $1^1/4$".
- Cut 2 **upper strap interfacings** 22" x $1^1/4$".

PREPARING THE QUILTED SECTIONS

*Follow **Sewing**, page 73, and **Pressing**, page 75. Match right sides and raw edges and use a ¹/₄" seam allowance.*

1. Mark center of 1 long edge of **front/side.** Mark center of 1 long edge of **bottom**.
2. Matching center marks, sew front/side and bottom together (**Fig. 1**). Press seam allowance toward **front/side**.

Fig. 1

3. Refer to **Making Quilted Fabric**, page 75, to layer and quilt as desired using **front/side/bottom lining, front/side/bottom batting,** and **front/side/bottom.**

Quilting Tip: Our fabric is quilted with an allover meandering pattern.

4. Trim lining and batting even with edges of front/side/bottom.
5. Repeat **Steps 3-4** using **flap lining, flap batting,** and **flap.**

Quilting Tip: Our flap is quilted with a diagonal grid pattern.

6. Repeat **Steps 3-4** using **back lining, back batting,** and **back.**

Quilting Tip: Our back is quilted with a diagonal grid pattern.

ATTACHING THE TRIM AND ACCENT STRIPS

1. Matching wrong sides, press **front trim strips** and **flap trim strips** in half lengthwise.
2. Sew 1 front trim strip to each long right side edge of **front/side accent** (**Fig. 2**) and 1 flap trim strip to each long right side edge of **flap accent** (**Fig. 3**).

Fig. 2

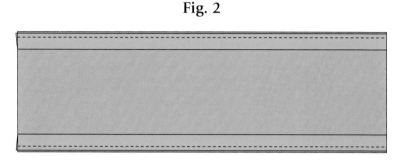

Fig. 3

3. Press front and flap trim strips away from front and flap accents (**Fig. 4**).

Fig. 4

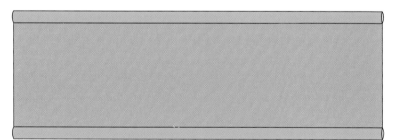

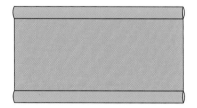

4. Position 1 edge of flap accent 1" from 1 short raw edge of flap. Using a walking foot, topstitch in place close to 1 folded edge of flap accent. Repeat for remaining folded edge (**Fig. 5**). If needed, trim ends of accent strips even with edges of flap.

Fig. 5

Quilting Tip: We added 1 straight line of quilting on each side of the medium stripe.

5. Repeat **Step 4** to attach front/side accent 1" above seamline on front/side/bottom.

Quilting Tip: We added 1 straight line of quilting on each side of the wide stripe.

PREPARING STRAPS, STRAP COVER, AND LOOP

1. Press 1 long and 1 short edge of each **upper** and **lower strap** ⅝" to wrong side.
2. On wrong side of 1 upper strap, align 1 long edge of 1 **upper strap interfacing** with long unpressed edge of strap. Tuck 1 short end of interfacing under folded short end. Stitch in place ¼" from long edge (**Fig. 6**).

Fig. 6

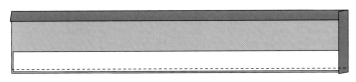

3. Fold interfacing over once, then fold pressed edge of handle over interfacing (**Figs. 7-8**).

Fig. 7

Fig. 8

4. Topstitch handle in place close to folded edge. Topstitch along length of opposite side of handle. Topstitch ⅛" outside each topstitching line (**Fig. 9**).

Fig. 9

5. Repeat **Steps 2-4** using remaining upper strap and upper strap interfacing and lower straps and lower strap interfacings.
6. Attach D-rings to the upper straps by placing finished end of strap through D-rings. Fold end of strap 2¼" to the wrong side and topstitch in place (**Fig. 10**).

Fig. 10

7. Leaving an opening for turning, sew **strap covers** together along all 4 sides (**Fig. 11**). Turn to right side; press.

Fig. 11

8. Press each edge of **loop** ¼" to the wrong side. Matching wrong sides, fold loop in half lengthwise and topstitch folded edges together.

ASSEMBLING THE BACKPACK

1. Press both long edges of each **long casing** 1/4" to wrong side. Press 1 short edge 1/4" to wrong side twice. To hem, topstitch across each pressed short edge.

2. Press both long edges of **short casing** 1/4" to wrong side. Mark center of top edge of front/ side/bottom. Center short casing over front/ side/bottom center mark 1/4" from top edge and top stitch in place along pressed edges (**Fig. 12**).

Fig. 12

3. With hemmed short edges over short casing, pin long casings to front/side 1/4" below top edge. Topstitch in place along pressed edges (**Fig. 13**).

Fig. 13

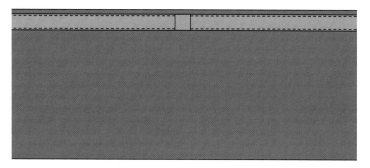

4. Fold **drawstring** in half to find and mark center. To prevent cord from fraying, wrap a length of tape around drawstring on either side of center mark. Cut drawstring in half at center mark. Insert 1 drawstring through each casing. To secure, stitch across ends at side edges (**Fig. 14**).

Fig. 14

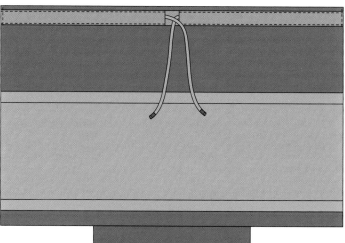

5. Mark center top on 1 short edge of **back**. With ends of **loop** even with top raw edge, baste loop to right side of back about $^3/_8$" on either side of center mark (**Fig. 15**).

Strap Diagram

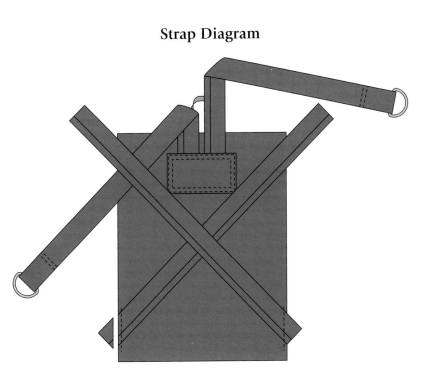

Fig. 15

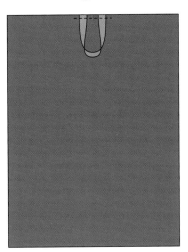

6. Referring to **Strap Diagram**, center and sew raw ends of upper straps to right side of back 3" below top edge.

7. Center strap cover over raw ends of upper straps and topstitch in place around all 4 sides. Topstitch again $^1/_4$" inside previous stitching.

8. Position raw ends of lower straps at a 45° angle, 1" above bottom edge of back. Stitch in place. Trim ends of straps even with side edges of back.

9. To make inner pocket, match wrong sides and short ends and fold **inner pocket** in half. Fold lower folded edge up 4" (**Fig. 16**). Baste layers together along sides.

Fig. 16

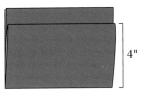

4"

10. Refer to **Making Binding**, page 77, to make **binding** using **binding strips**.

11. To bind side edges of pocket, refer to **Attaching Closed End Binding**, page 78, for lower edges and **Attaching Open End Binding**, page 78, for upper edges.

12. Center top edge of pocket on lining side of back. Baste in place along upper edge.

13. Matching right sides and top raw edges, sew back and flap together. Refer to **Attaching Open End Binding**, page 78, to use prepared binding to bind top edge of back.

14. Press under both long edges of **back trim strip** $^1/_4$" to the wrong side. On right side of back, position back trim strip over seam and loop ends. Topstitch along both pressed edges of trim strip.

15. Matching right sides, sew 1 side edge of bottom to 1 bottom edge of front/side (**Fig. 17**). Repeat for remaining side. Refer to **Attaching Closed End Binding**, page 78, to use prepared binding to bind seam end at front of bag and **Attaching Open end Binding**, page 78, to bind seam end at back of bag.

16. Matching right sides, refer to **Fig. 18** to pin then sew back to front/side around all 3 sides. Refer to **Attaching Open End Binding**, page 78, to use prepared binding to bind seam allowances.

Fig. 18

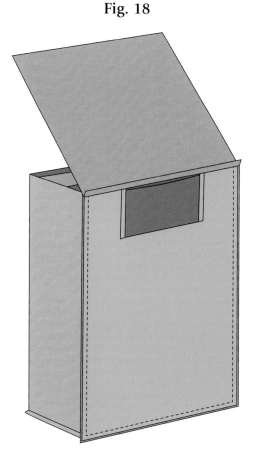

Fig. 17

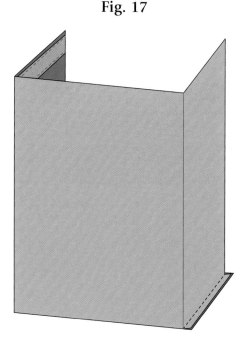

17. Referring to **Fig. 19**, use a small drinking glass (approximately 3" in diameter) to round corners of flap.

Fig. 19

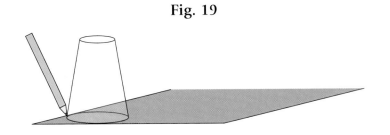

18. Refer to **Attaching Continuous Binding**, page 77, to use prepared binding to bind remaining raw edges of top edge and flap (**Fig. 20**).

Fig. 20

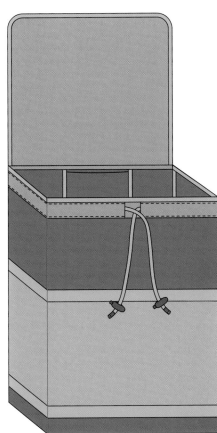

19. To attach cord stops to drawstring ends, depress top of cord stop and thread 1 drawstring end through hole. Repeat for remaining cord stop and drawstring.

bongo
BAG

Musical instruments, bike gear, beach towels—if you need to get mobile with bulky materials, this bag is your best bet. And if you're a dyed-in-the-cotton quilter, the four-patch exterior gives you a moving billboard for showcasing favorite fabrics.

Finished Size: 8" x 19" x 8" (20 cm x 48 cm x 20 cm)

SUPPLIES

Yardage is based on 43"/44" (109 cm/112 cm) wide fabric.

$1^3/_8$ yds (1.3 m) of red tone-on-tone print fabric
$1/_8$ yd (11 cm) **each** of 4 assorted print fabrics
$1/_4$ yd (23 cm) of black floral fabric

You will also need:

$37^1/_2$" x $17^1/_2$" (95 cm x 44 cm) rectangle of lightweight batting (we used Warm and Natural®)
1 yard (91 cm) of Pellon® Peltex®70 heavyweight interfacing
3 yds (2.7 m) of $1/_4$" (6 mm) dia. braided cord for drawstring
Ten $1/_4$" (6 mm) dia. eyelets

CUTTING THE PIECES

*Follow **Rotary Cutting**, page 72, to cut fabric. Cut all strips across the selvage-to-selvage width of the fabric. All measurements include ¹/₄" seam allowances.*

From red tone-on-tone fabric:
- Cut 1 **lining** 37¹/₂" x 17¹/₂".
- Cut 2 **bottom squares** 9" x 9".
- Cut 2 **binding strips** 2¹/₂" wide.
- Cut 11 **squares** 5¹/₂" x 5¹/₂".
- Cut 2 **upper bands** 2¹/₂" x 35¹/₂".

From *each* assorted print fabric:
- Cut 1 **strip** 3" wide.

From black floral fabric:
- Cut 2 **lower bands** 4" x 35¹/₂".

From interfacing:
- Cut 1 **upper band interfacing** 1¹/₂" x 34".
- Cut 1 **lower band interfacing** 3" x 34".
- Cut 1 **bottom interfacing** 7¹/₂" x 7¹/₂".

MAKING THE BAG BODY

*Follow **Sewing**, page 73, and **Pressing**, page 75. Match right sides and raw edges and use a ¹/₄" seam allowance unless otherwise stated.*

1. Sew 2 **strips** together to make **Strip Set A**. Cut across Strip Set A at 3" intervals to make 10 Unit 1's.

Strip Set A

Unit 1
(make 10)

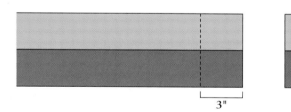

3"

2. Sew remaining strips together to make **Strip Set B**. Cut across Strip Set B at 3" intervals to make 10 Unit 2's.

Strip Set B

Unit 2
(make 10)

3"

3. Sew 1 Unit 1 and 1 Unit 2 together to make **Four-Patch Block**. Make 10 Four-Patch Blocks.

Four-Patch Block
(make 10)

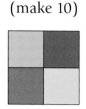

4. Sew 4 **squares** and 3 Four-Patch Blocks together to make Row 1. Make 2 Row 1's.
5. Sew 4 Four-Patch Blocks and 3 squares together to make Row 2.
6. Sew Rows together to make **bag body**.

Bag Body

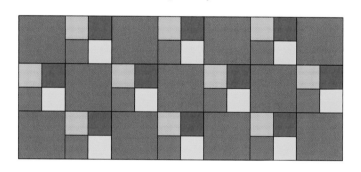

7. Refer to **Making Quilted Fabric**, page 75, to layer and quilt as desired using **bag body**, **batting rectangle**, and **lining**.

Quilting Tip: Our bag body is quilted in the ditch between the Rows and with a diagonal grid pattern.

8. Trim batting and lining even with edges of bag body.

ASSEMBLING THE BAG

1. Center and layer 1 **bottom square** (wrong side up), **bottom interfacing**, and remaining **bottom square** (wrong side down). Stitch an X through the center of the layered square. Baste layers together around outer edges. Set aside.

2. Matching right sides and long edges, sew 1 **upper band** to 1 long edge of bag body (**Fig. 1**).

Fig. 1

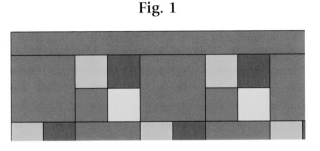

3. Press 1 long edge of remaining **upper band** 1/4" to the wrong side; unfold. Center **upper band interfacing** on wrong side of upper band with 1 long edge of interfacing butted against fold line of band (**Fig. 2**). Baste interfacing in place along all edges.

Fig. 2

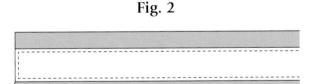

4. Matching right sides and long raw edges, use a 1/2" seam allowance to sew upper bands together (**Fig. 3**).

Fig. 3

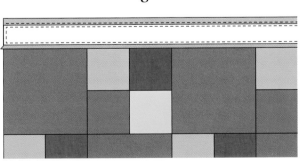

5. Center **lower band interfacing** on wrong side of 1 **lower band** (**Fig. 4**). Baste interfacing in place.

Fig. 4

6. Matching long raw edges, layer interfaced lower band (right side up), bag body (right side up), and remaining lower band (wrong side up). Sew layers together using a 1/2" seam allowance. Press lower bands toward bottom edge of bag body covering seam allowance. Topstitch close to top edge of lower band. Topstitch 1/4" away from first topstitching line (**Fig. 5**).

Fig. 5

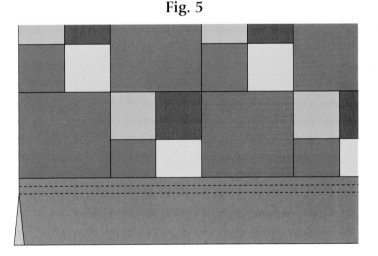

7. Refer to **Fig. 6** to mark position of eyelets on upper and lower bands. Follow manufacturer's instructions to attach eyelets on lower band **only**.

Fig. 6

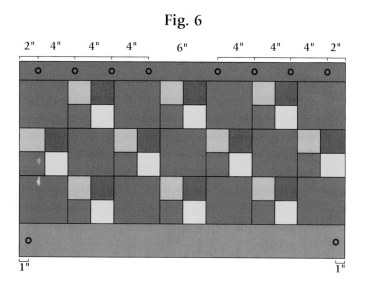

8. Unfold pressed top edge of upper band. Sew center back seam from bottom of bag through both upper bands.

9. Refer to **Making Binding**, page 77, to make binding using binding strips. Refer to **Attaching Open End Binding**, page 78, to bind seam allowance, stopping binding just above the seam between the bag body and upper band. **Do not** bind to top edge.

10. Re-fold pressed top edge of upper band. Fold upper band to the inside of bag covering top raw edge of binding and seam allowances; pin. Topstitch close to both the top and bottom edges of upper band. Topstitch $1/4$" inside each outer topstitching line.

11. Follow manufacturer's instructions to attach eyelets at marks on upper band.

12. To attach bag bottom, mark the 4 corners of the bag by measuring 4" from either side of back seam along bottom edge; place pins. Measure 8" from these pins and place pins in these 2 locations (**Fig 7**). With wrong side of bag facing out, align corners of bottom with pins in bag; pin bottom to bag along all 4 sides.

Fig. 7

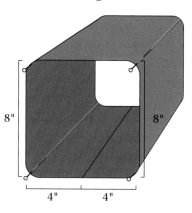

13. Attach a zipper foot and select far left needle position. Easing as needed and stopping with needle down to pivot at corner pins, use a $1/2"$ seam allowance to sew from corner pin to corner pin around bottom. Reinforce seam by zigzagging in the seam allowance, close to the first line of stitching. Refer to **Attaching Continuous Binding**, page 77, to use prepared binding to bind seam allowance. Turn bag right side out.

Tip: To make sewing around the bottom corners easier, you can "scrunch" the lower band of the bag as needed. The interfacing will spring back to its original shape once released.

14. To attach drawstring, knot one end of drawstring. Working from inside bag to outside, thread unknotted end through one bottom eyelet. Thread the end from outside to inside through the upper eyelet on the same side of back seam. Weave drawstring in and out of remaining upper eyelets. Thread end of drawstring through remaining lower eyelet from outside to inside. Knot end; tie knotted ends together.

weekender
DUFFLE BAG

Weekender? Yes, there are two good reasons for its name. The first is, you can sew it in a weekend. The second is a bit more obvious: it's the perfect grab-and-go bag to get you and all your gear away for a couple days of fun. With a wide zipper closure and two generous side pockets, it can take on an active weekend with a rare combination of practicality and style.

Finished Size: 25" x 14" x 12" (64 cm x 36 cm x 30 cm)

SUPPLIES

Yardage is based on 43"/44" (109 cm/112 cm) wide fabric.
   2 1/2 yds (2.3 m) of black floral fabric
   1/4 yd (23 cm) **each** of 3 coordinating fabrics for pockets
   2 1/2 yds (2.3 m) of purple print fabric
You will also need:
   47" x 68" (119 cm x 173 cm) rectangle of thin batting (we used
     Warm and Natural®)
   1 yd (91 cm) of Pellon® Peltex®70 heavyweight interfacing
   Quilt basting spray
   24" (61 cm) plastic zipper

CUTTING THE PIECES

*Follow **Rotary Cutting**, page 72, to cut fabric. Cut all strips across the selvage-to-selvage width of the fabric. All measurements include 1/4" seam allowances.*

From black floral fabric:
- Cut 1 **outer fabric** 27" x 64".
- Cut 2 **handle accents** 2¹/₂" x 60".
- Cut 5 **binding strips** 2¹/₂" wide.
- Cut 4 **front/back trim strips** 2" x 25¹/₂".
- Cut 2 **zipper end covers** 1¹/₂" x 3".

From *each* of 3 coordinating fabrics:
- Cut 2 **strips** 2¹/₂" wide.

From purple print fabric:
- Cut 1 **bag lining** 29" x 66".
- Cut 2 **handles** 3¹/₈" x 60".
- Cut 2 **pocket linings** 15¹/₂" x 15¹/₂".

From batting:
- Cut 1 **bag batting** 29" x 66".
- Cut 2 **pocket battings** 15¹/₂" x 15¹/₂".

From interfacing:
- Cut 4 **handle interfacings** 1¹/₂" x 30".

PREPARING THE HANDLES

1. Cut 2 **handle interfacings** in half to make four 1¹/₂" x 15" pieces.
2. Piece handle interfacings together in the order shown (**Fig. 1**). Butt (do not overlap) edges against each other and zigzag. Repeat for remaining handle.

Fig. 1

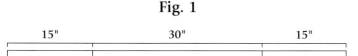

3. Press both long edges of each **handle accent** 1/2" to wrong side; unfold pressed edges.
4. Aligning long edges of handle interfacing with folds in handle accent, place 1 handle interfacing on wrong side of 1 handle accent. Fold pressed edges over interfacing. Baste interfacing in place down the middle (**Fig. 2**). Repeat for remaining handle.

Fig. 2

5. Press 1 long edge of each **handle** 5/8" to the wrong side.
6. Matching wrong sides, center and pin 1 handle accent over 1 handle. Topstitch on each side of handle accent close to folded edges. Topstitch 1/4" inside each outer topstitching line. Repeat for remaining handle. Set handles aside.

PREPARING THE BAG SECTIONS

1. Refer to **Making Binding**, page 77, to use **binding strips** to make **binding**. Set binding aside.
2. Refer to **Making Quilted Fabric**, page 75, to layer and quilt as desired using **outer fabric**, **bag batting**, and **bag lining**.

Quilting Tip: Our fabric is quilted with an allover meandering pattern.

3. Cut quilted fabric into 2 **front/back rectangles** 25" x 24" and 2 **side rectangles** 14" x 12" (**Fig. 3**).

Fig. 3

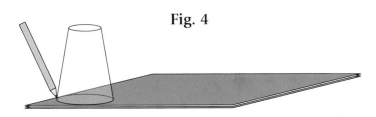

4. Refer to **Attaching Open End Binding**, page 78, to use prepared binding to bind one long edge of each front/back rectangle. Set front/back rectangles aside.

5. Referring **Fig. 4**, use a small drinking glass (approximately 3" in diameter) to round each corner of 1 side rectangle. Repeat for remaining side rectangle. Set side rectangles aside.

Fig. 4

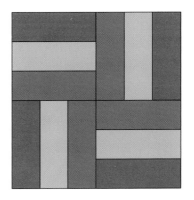

MAKING THE POCKETS

Follow Sewing, page 73, and Pressing, page 75. Match right sides and raw edges and use a ¹/₄" seam allowance.

1. Sew 1 **strip** of each coordinating fabric together to make **Strip Set**. Make 2 Strip Sets. Cut across Strip Sets at 6¹/₂" intervals to make 8 **Unit 1's**.

Strip Set
(make 2)

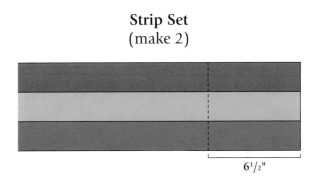

6¹/₂"

Unit 1
(make 8)

2. Sew 4 Unit 1's together to make **pieced pocket**. Make 2 pieced pockets.

Pieced Pocket
(make 2)

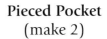

3. Refer to **Making Quilted Fabric**, page 75, to layer and quilt as desired using **pocket linings**, **pocket battings**, and **pieced pockets**.

Quilting Tip: Our pockets are quilted in the ditch along the seamlines.

4. Trim batting and lining even with pieced pockets to make **pockets**.
5. Refer to **Attaching Open End Binding**, page 78, to use prepared binding to bind 1 edge of each pocket. Set pockets aside.

ASSEMBLING THE BAG

1. With zipper closed, refer to **Fig. 5** to position right side of **zipper end covers** on right side of zipper approximately 21½" apart. Sew across zipper and zipper end covers through all layers.

Fig 5

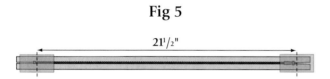

2. Matching wrong sides and short edges, fold zipper end covers in half and press.
3. Center bound edge of 1 front/back rectangle over one side of zipper. Using a zipper foot, topstitch bound edge of front/back rectangle to zipper as close to zipper as possible. Topstitch again ¼" from first topstitching. Repeat for remaining front/back to make **bag body** (**Fig. 6**).

Fig 6

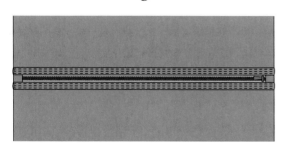

4. With bound edge of pocket facing zipper, center 1 pocket on each side of bag body, 6½" from bound edge of bag body; pin. Baste ¼" from the sides and bottom edges of the pockets (**Fig. 7**). This will prevent pockets from shifting when attaching handles.

Fig. 7

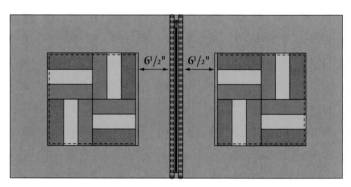

5. Pin handles on each side of pockets with handle accent facing up, covering raw edges and overlapping pockets by ¼". Topstitch in place over previous outer topstitching.
6. Refer to **Fig. 8** to topstitch a small rectangle at top of pocket for reinforcement.

Fig. 8

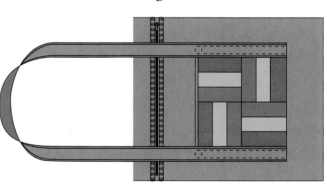

7. Matching right sides and long edges, press **front/back trim strips** in half. Position raw edge of 1 front/back trim strip across bag body ¹/₄" below bottom edge of 1 pocket. Using a ¹/₄" seam allowance, stitch trim strip to bag body (**Fig. 9**). Fold trim strip up to cover raw edge of pocket. Topstitch in place close to folded edge (**Fig. 10**). Repeat for remaining front/back trim strip.

Fig. 9   Fig. 10

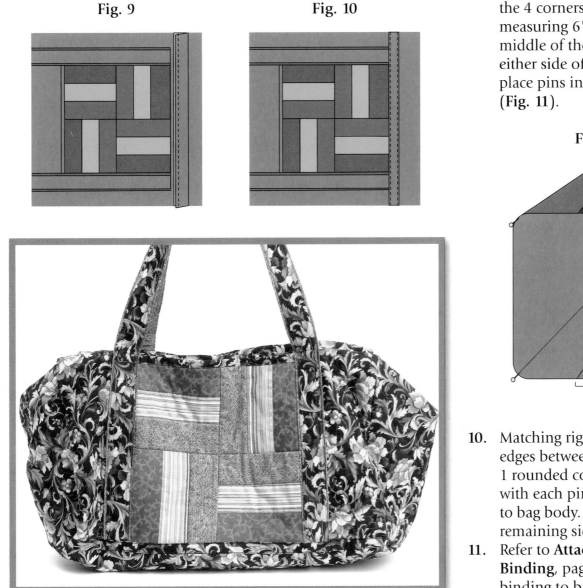

8. Matching right sides and short raw edges, sew bottom seam. Refer to **Attaching Open End Binding**, page 78, to use prepared binding to bind bottom seam allowances.

9. To attach **side rectangles**, turn bag body wrong side out. Mark the 4 corners of bag body by measuring 6" on each side of the middle of the zipper and 6" on either side of the bottom seam; place pins in these 4 locations (**Fig. 11**).

Fig. 11

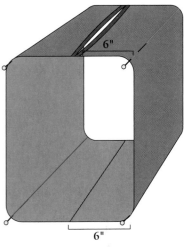

6"

6"

10. Matching right sides and short edges between pins, align 1 rounded corner of side rectangle with each pin. Sew side rectangle to bag body. Repeat to attach remaining side.

11. Refer to **Attaching Continuous Binding**, page 77, to use prepared binding to bind seam allowances.

project
PATTERNS

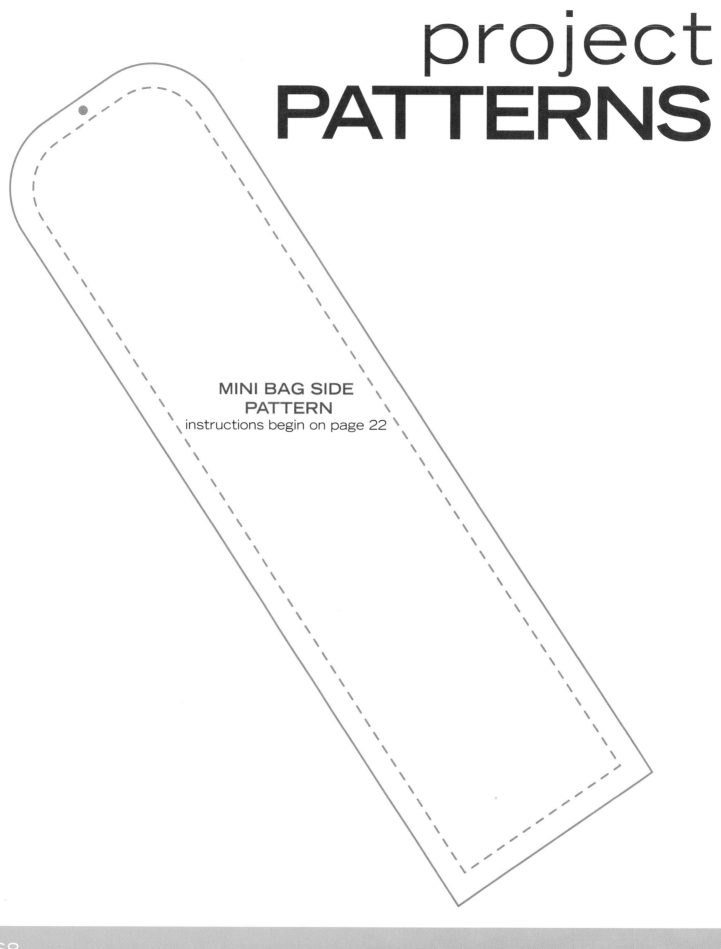

**MINI BAG SIDE
PATTERN**
instructions begin on page 22

**SHOULDER BAG FRONT/BACK
PATTERN**
instructions begin on page 38

Fold

To trace a complete pattern, trace half the pattern
onto tracing paper using a pen or pencil with dark lead.
Fold tracing paper in half along fold line, flip paper to
unmarked side and trace along previously drawn lines.

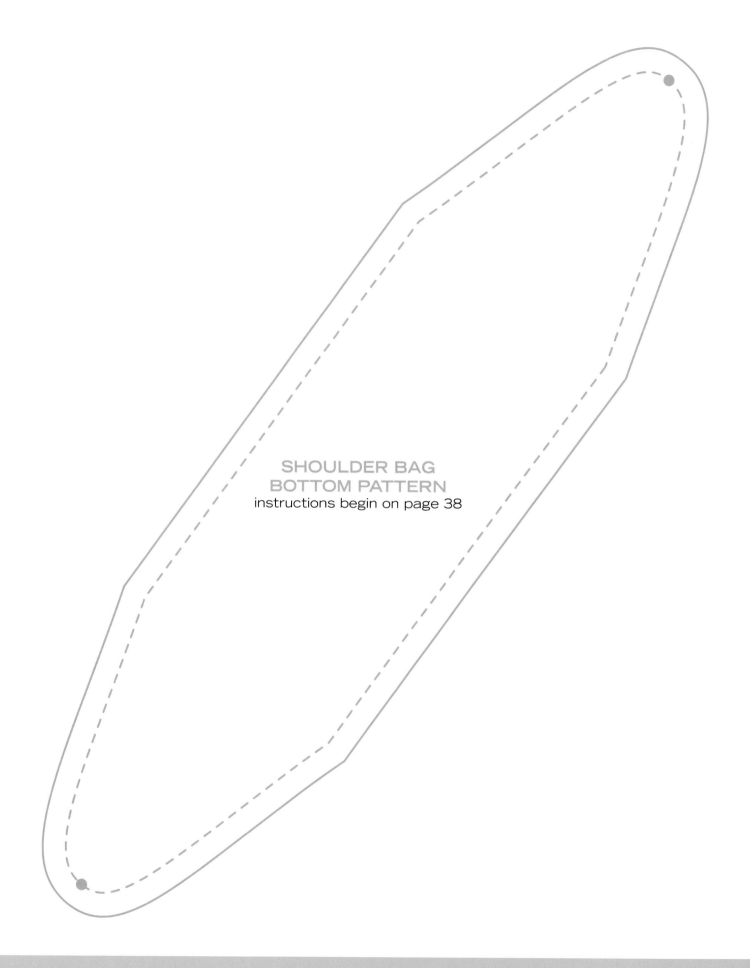

SHOULDER BAG
BOTTOM PATTERN
instructions begin on page 38

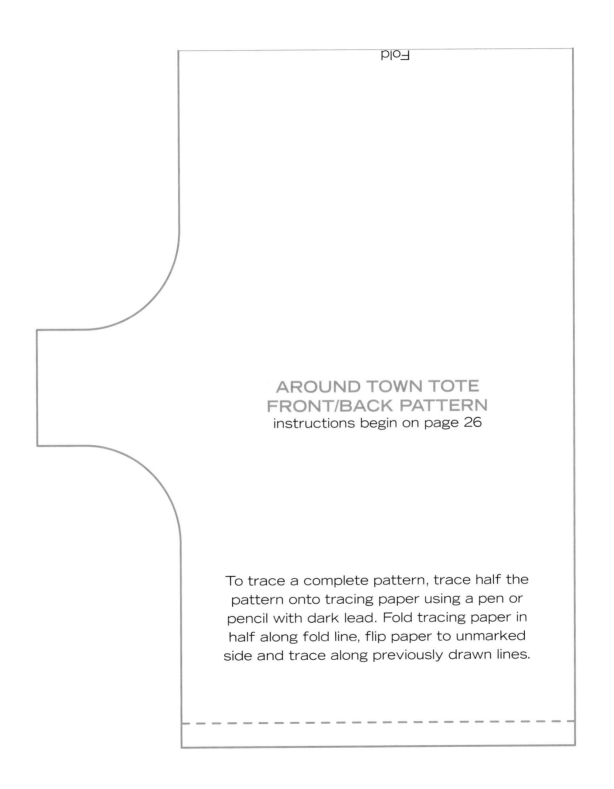

Fold

**AROUND TOWN TOTE
FRONT/BACK PATTERN**
instructions begin on page 26

To trace a complete pattern, trace half the
pattern onto tracing paper using a pen or
pencil with dark lead. Fold tracing paper in
half along fold line, flip paper to unmarked
side and trace along previously drawn lines.

general INSTRUCTIONS

To make your sewing and quilting easier and more enjoyable, we encourage you to carefully read all of the general instructions, study the color photographs, and familiarize yourself with the individual project instructions before beginning a project.

FABRICS

SELECTING FABRICS
Choose high-quality, medium-weight 100% cotton fabrics. All-cotton fabrics hold a crease better, fray less, and are easier to quilt than cotton/polyester blends.
Yardage requirements listed for each project are based on 43"/44" wide fabric with a "usable" width of 40" after shrinkage and trimming selvages. Actual usable width will probably vary slightly from fabric to fabric. Our recommended yardage lengths should be adequate for occasional re-squaring of fabric when many cuts are required.

PREPARING FABRICS
We recommend that all fabrics be washed, dried, and pressed before cutting. If fabrics are not pre-washed, washing the finished project will cause shrinkage and give it a more "antiqued" look and feel. Bright and dark colors, which may run, should always be washed before cutting. After washing and drying fabric, fold lengthwise with wrong sides together and matching selvages.

ROTARY CUTTING
Most of the pieces for the projects are rotary cut. In many cases you will make a first cut across the width of the fabric, then cut that strip into the final size(s).

- Make all cuts from the selvage-to-selvage width of the fabric unless otherwise indicated in project instructions.

- Place fabric on work surface with fold closest to you.

- Square left edge of fabric using rotary cutter and rulers (**Figs. 1 - 2**).

Fig. 1

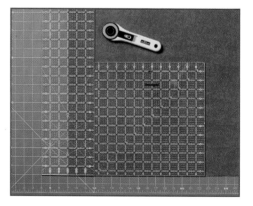

Fig. 2

- To cut each strip required for a project, place ruler over cut edge of fabric, aligning desired marking on ruler with cut edge; make cut (**Fig. 3**).

Fig. 3

- When cutting several strips from a single piece of fabric, it is important to make sure that cuts remain at a perfect right angle to the fold; square fabric as needed.
- Remove selvage edges before sub-cutting strips to final sizes.

SEWING
Precise cutting, followed by accurate sewing, will ensure that all pieces of your project fit together well.

- Set sewing machine stitch length for approximately 11 stitches per inch.

- Use a matching or neutral-colored 100% cotton sewing thread (not quilting thread) in needle and in bobbin.

- An accurate seam allowance is essential.

- When sewing, always place pieces right sides together and match raw edges, unless otherwise indicated; pin if necessary.

PIECING
Sewing small fabric shapes, such as squares, triangles, or rectangles, together to form larger shapes is called Piecing. For example, the pockets of the **Star Sampler Tote***, page 6, are pieced. Piecing requires the use of some specific techniques not usually found in basic sewing.*

Trimming Points
Trim away points of any seam allowances that extend beyond edges of sewn pieces (**Fig. 4**).

Fig. 4

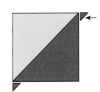

Sewing Across Seam Intersections

When sewing across intersection of two seams, place pieces right sides together and match seams exactly, making sure seam allowances are pressed in opposite directions (**Fig. 5**).

Fig. 5

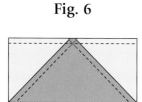

Sewing Sharp Points

To ensure sharp points when joining triangular or diagonal pieces, stitch across the center of the "X" (shown in pink) formed on wrong side by previous seams (**Fig. 6**).

Fig. 6

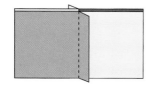

Making Triangle-Squares

This method reduces handling of the bias edges that is normally required when triangles are cut then sewn. If you prefer a different method, please use it!

1. Matching right sides and raw edges, place two squares together. On the wrong side of the lighter colored square, draw a diagonal line across the square (**Fig. 7**).

Fig. 7

2. Sew $1/4$" from each side of drawn line (**Fig. 8**).

Fig. 8

3. Cut on drawn line to make 2 **Triangle-Squares** (**Fig. 9**).

Fig. 9

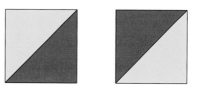

4. Press seam allowances toward darker fabric and trim, if needed, to the size given in project instructions (**Fig. 10**).

Fig. 10

PRESSING

- Use steam iron set on "Cotton" for all pressing.

- Press after sewing each seam.

PRESSING WHEN PIECING

- Seam allowances are almost always pressed to one side, usually toward darker fabric. However, to reduce bulk it may occasionally be necessary to press seam allowances toward the lighter fabric or even to press them open.

- To prevent dark fabric seam allowances from showing through light fabric, it may occasionally be necessary to trim darker seam allowance slightly narrower than lighter seam allowance.

MAKING QUILTED FABRIC

*Quilting holds the three layers (outer fabric, batting, and lining) of a quilt "sandwich" together. Our projects are machine quilted. Please read entire **Making Quilted Fabric** section, pages 75 – 76, before beginning project.*

TYPES OF QUILTING DESIGNS

Some quilting designs need to be marked on the fabric. Depending on the design this can be done before or after basting the layers together.

In the Ditch Quilting

Quilting along seamlines is called "in the ditch" quilting. This type of quilting should be done on side **opposite** seam allowance and does not have to be marked.

Outline Quilting

Quilting a consistent distance, usually $1/4$", from seam is called "outline" quilting. Outline quilting may be marked, or $1/4$" masking tape may be placed along seamlines for quilting guide. (Do not leave tape on quilt longer than necessary, since it may leave an adhesive residue.)

Channel Quilting

Quilting with straight, parallel lines is called "channel" quilting. This type of quilting may be marked or you can use a guide such as 1"-2" wide masking tape.

Crosshatch Quilting

Quilting straight lines in a grid pattern is called "crosshatch" quilting. Lines may be stitched parallel to edges of the quilt sandwich or stitched diagonally. This type of quilting may be marked or you can use a guide such as 1"-2" wide masking tape.

Meandering Quilting

Free-motion quilting in random curved lines and swirls is called "meandering" quilting. Quilting lines should not cross or touch each other. This type of quilting does not need to be marked.

MARKING QUILTING LINES

Quilting lines may be marked using fabric marking pencils, chalk markers, water- or air-soluble pens, or lead pencils.

Simple quilting designs may be marked with chalk or chalk pencil after making the quilt sandwich. A small area may be marked, then quilted, before moving to next area to be marked. Intricate designs should be marked before making the quilt sandwich using a more durable marker.

Caution: Pressing may permanently set some marks. **Test** different markers **on scrap fabric** to find one that marks clearly and can be thoroughly removed.

MAKING THE QUILT SANDWICH

1. Cover work area with paper or plastic to prevent damage from overspray.
2. Position **lining** wrong side up on a flat work surface. Following manufacturer's instructions, spray lining lightly with quilt basting spray. Place **batting** over lining and smooth pieces together.
3. Lightly spray wrong side of **outer fabric** with quilt basting spray. Position outer fabric, right side up, over batting and smooth pieces together. Press layers together firmly with your hands.

MACHINE QUILTING METHODS

Thread the needle with general-purpose thread that matches the outer fabric to make quilting lines blend with the outer fabric or use a decorative thread, such as a variegated, a metallic, or a contrasting-color general-purpose thread, to make quilting lines stand out more. Use general-purpose thread in bobbin. **Do not** use quilting thread.

Tip: When quilting, start in the middle of the quilt sandwich and work your way to the outer edges.

Straight-Line Quilting

The term "straight-line" is somewhat deceptive, since curves (especially gentle ones) as well as straight lines can be stitched with this technique.

1. Set stitch length for six to ten stitches per inch and attach walking foot to sewing machine.
2. Determine which section of the quilt sandwich will have longest continuous quilting line, oftentimes this will be from corner to corner when crosshatching. Roll up and secure each edge of a large quilt sandwich to help reduce the bulk. Smaller quilt sandwiches may not need to be rolled.

3. Begin stitching on longest quilting line, using very short stitches for the first $1/4$" to "lock" quilting. Stitch across quilt sandwich, using one hand on each side of walking foot to slightly spread fabric and to guide fabric through machine. Lock stitches at end of quilting line.
4. Continue machine quilting, stitching longer quilting lines first to stabilize the quilt sandwich before moving on to other areas.

Free-Motion Quilting

Free-motion quilting may be free form or may follow a marked pattern. Meandering is a type of free-motion quilting.

1. Attach darning foot to sewing machine and lower or cover feed dogs.
2. Position quilt sandwich under the darning foot; lower foot. Holding top thread, take a stitch and pull bobbin thread to top of quilt sandwich. To "lock" beginning of quilting line, hold top and bobbin threads while making three to five stitches in place.
3. Use one hand on each side of darning foot to slightly spread fabric and to move quilt sandwich through the machine. Even stitch length is achieved by using smooth, flowing hand motion and steady machine speed. Slow machine speed and fast hand movement will create long stitches. Fast machine speed and slow hand movement will create short stitches. Move quilt sandwich sideways, back and forth, in a circular motion, or in a random motion to create desired designs; do not rotate quilt sandwich. Lock stitches at end of each quilting line.

BINDING

Binding is used to cover raw edges to give a finished look to your project.

MAKING BINDING

1. Use the diagonal seams method (**Fig. 11**), to sew binding strips together end to end to make 1 continuous binding strip.

Fig. 11

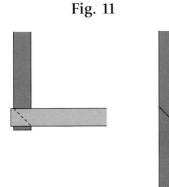

2. Matching wrong sides and raw edges, press strips in half lengthwise to complete binding.

ATTACHING BINDING

For any of the following methods of attaching binding, you will first sew the raw edges of the binding to the "wrong" or lining side of the project and bring the folded edge to the "right" or outer fabric side and topstitch in place (**Fig. 12**).

Fig. 12

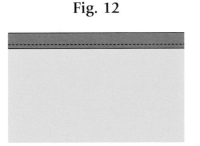

Sometimes this is obvious like the binding around the top edge of the **Star Sampler Tote**, page 6. The lining is the wrong side and the outer fabric is the right side. Other times the right and wrong sides are not quite as apparent such as around the flap and outer edges of the **Mini Bag**, page 22. In this case, the outer fabric of the side and the lining of the flap would be the wrong side and the outer fabric of the project body is the right side. When binding seams on the inside of a project, it doesn't matter which side of the seam allowance you use as the right side.

ATTACHING CONTINUOUS BINDING

Continuous Binding has no easily visible beginning or end and is used around the edges of a bag, wallet, or tote.

1. Press 1 end of binding diagonally (**Fig. 13**).

Fig. 13

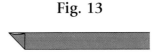

2. Beginning on wrong/lining side of project with the pressed end of binding, match raw edges of project and binding and pin binding around raw edge of project.
3. Using a $1/4$" seam allowance, sew binding to project, until binding overlaps beginning end by about 2". Trim excess binding.
4. Fold binding to right side, covering stitching line and pin in place.
5. Topstitch binding in place close to folded edge.

ATTACHING OPEN END BINDING

Open End Binding is used when the raw ends of a bound edge will be caught in a seam or covered by another strip of binding.

1. Matching raw edges of binding to raw edge of project, pin a length of binding along one edge. Using a $1/4$" seam allowance, sew binding to project (**Fig. 14**).

Fig. 14

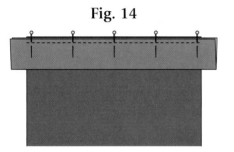

2. Fold binding over seam allowance, covering stitching line, and pin pressed edge in place (**Fig. 15**).

Fig. 15

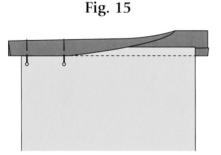

3. Topstitch binding in place close to pressed edge.
4. Trim raw ends of binding even with edges.

ATTACHING CLOSED END BINDING

Closed End Binding is used when the seam to be bound will not be caught or covered by another seam. **Note:** *In some cases, a project, such as **Star Sampler Tote**, page 6, may have a bound top edge and no bottom seam. You may need to use the Closed End Binding method on the end of the side seam allowance closest to the project bottom and the Open End method on the end closest to the top edge.*

1. Matching raw edges and leaving approximately $1/2$" of binding extending at end(s), pin a length of binding along one edge (**Fig. 16**).

Fig. 16

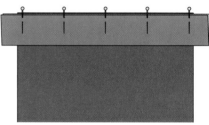

2. Using a $1/4$" seam allowance, sew binding to project (**Fig. 17**).

Fig. 17

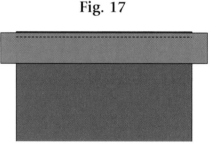

3. Fold under raw end(s) of binding (**Fig. 18**); pin in place. Fold binding over seam allowance, covering stitching line, and pin pressed edge in place (**Fig. 19**).

Fig. 18

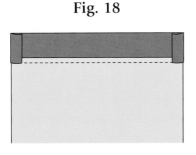

Fig. 19

4. Topstitch binding in place close to pressed edge.

ATTACHING BINDING WITH MITERED CORNERS

*Mitered Corners are used when you have 90° angles to bind, such as the corners on the **Quilted Wallet**, page 34.*

1. Press 1 end of binding diagonally (**Fig. 20**).

Fig. 20

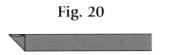

2. Beginning with pressed end several inches from a corner, lay binding around project to make sure that seams in binding will not end up at a corner. Adjust placement if necessary. Pin binding to project along one side.

3. When you reach the first corner, mark $1/4$" from corner (**Fig. 21**).

Fig. 21

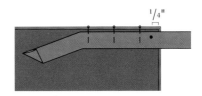

4. Using a $1/4$" seam allowance, sew binding to project, backstitching at beginning of stitching and at mark (**Fig. 22**). Lift needle out of fabric and clip thread.

Fig. 22

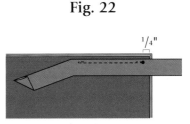

5. Fold binding as shown in **Figs. 23 – 24** and pin binding to adjacent side, matching raw edges. When you've reached the next corner, mark $1/4$" from edge of project.

Fig. 23

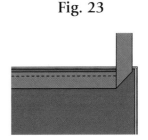

Fig. 24

6. Backstitching at edge of project, sew pinned binding to project (**Fig. 25**); backstitch at the next mark. Lift needle out of fabric and clip thread.

Fig. 25

7. Continue sewing binding to project, until binding overlaps beginning end by about 2". Trim excess binding.

8. On one edge of project, fold binding over, covering stitching line and pin in place (**Fig. 26**). On adjacent side, fold binding over, forming a mitered corner. Repeat for each corner. Fold and pin remaining binding (**Fig. 27**).

Fig. 26

Fig. 27

9. Topstitch binding in place close to folded edge.

Metric Conversion Chart	
Inches x 2.54 = centimeters (cm)	Yards x .9144 = meters (m)
Inches x 25.4 = millimeters (mm)	Yards x 91.44 = centimeters (cm)
Inches x .0254 = meters (m)	Centimeters x .3937 = inches (")
	Meters x 1.0936 = yards (yd)

Standard Equivalents					
1/8"	3.2 mm	0.32 cm	1/8 yard	11.43 cm	0.11 m
1/4"	6.35 mm	0.635 cm	1/4 yard	22.86 cm	0.23 m
3/8"	9.5 mm	0.95 cm	3/8 yard	34.29 cm	0.34 m
1/2"	12.7 mm	1.27 cm	1/2 yard	45.72 cm	0.46 m
5/8"	15.9 mm	1.59 cm	5/8 yard	57.15 cm	0.57 m
3/4"	19.1 mm	1.91 cm	3/4 yard	68.58 cm	0.69 m
7/8"	22.2 mm	2.22 cm	7/8 yard	80 cm	0.8 m
1"	25.4 mm	2.54 cm	1 yard	91.44 cm	0.91 m